W9-DFK-782

CHILD WELFARE LEAGUE OF AMERICA

CWLA CHILD WELFARE LEAGUE OF AMERICA

STANDARDS FOR SERVICES FOR UNMARRIED PARENTS

REVISED: 1971

Child Welfare League of America, Inc.
67 Irving Place, New York, N.Y. 10003

2-18-86

Third Printing 1979

Library of Congress Catalog Card Number: 75-184509
ISBN: 0-87868-094-2

ACKNOWLEDGMENTS

This revision of the edition of the Child Welfare League of America Standards for Services for Unmarried Parents published in 1960 was prepared by a committee whose members, selected on the basis of their expertness in this field, represent affiliates of the League member agencies throughout this country and also from Canada, and other agencies, national organizations and professions concerned with services for unmarried parents and their children. The committee discussed suggestions for the revisions that were received from 174 member agencies, state and local departments of welfare, other organizations and consultants who were requested to review the first edition. The revised statement incorporates changes recommended by the committee and some additional suggestions made by 87 member agencies, state departments of welfare, other national organizations, and League staff and board members who reviewed the draft.

The Board of Directors of the Child Welfare League of America approved the revised statement of the *Standards for Services for Unmarried Parents* on June 8, 1971.

Committee on Revision of CWLA Standards for Services for Unmarried Parents

Chairman Mrs. Joyce P. Austin, Board of Directors, CWLA
Mrs. Sharon Beauregard, Children's Aid Society of Ottawa
Mary Alice Brogan, Children's Bureau of Delaware, Wilmington
Mrs. Ethel Carrington, Children's Services, Cleveland
Mrs. Charlotte S. Creighton, Northaven, Rochester, New York
Katherine Daly, Florence Crittenton Association of America, Chicago
Ezra C. Davidson, Jr., M.D., Charles R. Drew Post Graduate Medical School, Los Angeles
Alice M. Folsom, Child Welfare League of America, New York*
Ruth Friedman, National Council on Illegitimacy, New York*
Sister Marie Gaffney, M.S.B.T., National Conference of Catholic Charities, Washington
Ursula Gallagher, Office of Child Development, Department of Health, Education, and Welfare, Washington
Mrs. Elaine W. Grady, San Francisco Unified School District, San Francisco
Bertha Heinemeyer, Minnesota Department of Public Welfare, St. Paul
Betty Higley, Medina Children's Service, Seattle
Mrs. Gwendola Jones, Department of Health and Rehabilitative Services, Jacksonville, Florida
Mrs. Ann Lawton, Catholic Family Services, Hartford, Connecticut
Lt. Colonel Belle Leach, Volunteers of America, New York
Gertrud T. Mainzer, Esq., New York
Mrs. Doris McKelvy, Louise Wise Services, New York
Audrey J. McMaster, M.D., American College of Obstetricians and Gynecologists, Oklahoma City
Georgia L. McMurray, New York City Human Resources Administration, New York
Joyce Montgomery, R.N., American College of Obstetricians and Gynecologists, New York
Dr. Patricia Morisey, National Urban League, New York
Albert J. Morris, Child and Family Services of Michigan, Farmington, Michigan
Reuben Pannor, Vista Del Mar Child Care Service, Los Angeles
Howard Robinson, Los Angeles County Department of Public Social Services, Los Angeles
Kathleen Roche, Baltimore County Department of Social Services, Towson, Maryland
Betty Rushing, Hope Cottage–Children's Bureau, Dallas
Mrs. Thelma Thompson, Department of Health, Education and Welfare, Chicago
Mrs. Vivian E. Washington, National Alliance Concerned with School Age Parents, Baltimore

Morris A. Wessel, M.D., New Haven, Connecticut (American Academy of Pediatrics)
Mrs. Peggy Wood, Onondaga County Department of Health, Syracuse, New York

*Affiliation at time of committee membership

Staff Gloria T. Chevers, Standards Development

Committee on Standards, 1971
Board of Directors, Child Welfare League of America

IV

CONTENTS

Standards for Services for Unmarried Parents

FOREWORD

Setting standards and improving practice in all social services for children have been major functions of the Child Welfare League of America since its formation almost 40 years ago. The 1955 study of the League's function and program reaffirmed that

> "continued development of standards designed to be used as objectives or goals, based on tested knowledge and approved practice in the various fields of service, should be given high priority in the the League's program."

Standards point up assumptions that need to be tested, and offer clues for research to obtain the knowledge required to serve children better. As we come to know what the essentials are for the healthy growth of all children we must restate the responsibility of society that child welfare services discharge, to provide for the child who would otherwise lack them the conditions and opportunities favorable to the development, use and enjoyment of his individual capacities.

In 1955, the League undertook to formulate a series of standards for child welfare services in the light of what is known today about the developmental needs of children and tested, effective ways of serving them. These statements are in some instances a comprehensive revision of standards previously issued by the League, and in others, an initial publication. Their preparation has involved examination of current practices and the assumptions on which they are based; survey of professional literature and standards developed by other groups, such as community planning and state welfare departments; and study of the most recent scientific findings of social work and related fields, such as child development, education, mental health, psychology, medicine, psychiatry, sociology, genetics and anthropology, as they bear on child welfare practice.

Final formulations have followed extended discussion of principles and issues by a committee of experts in each service, the drafting of a preliminary statement, and a critical review by League member agencies and representatives of related professions and other national organizations.

The preparation of standards has had wider participation of local and national agency representatives than any other project in League history. A high proportion of member agencies, including state departments of welfare, have contributed professional time and money for travel expenses of staff assigned to regional committees, and have reviewed draft statements and made suggestions for revision. Seventeen other national organizations, including governmental and church-related agencies and professional associations in related fields, have taken part in overall planning and the work of the various committees. The project has provided an opportunity to *think* about what we are doing, to define objectives, to clarify concepts, and to affirm convictions about what we want for children and believe society should make it possible for them to have.

Use of Standards

These standards are intended to be goals for continuous improvement of services for children. They are not the criteria for accreditation for League membership, although they will be used as the basis for establishing membership requirements. They represent practices considered to be most desirable in providing the social services that the community offers through various agencies out of its concern for children, to help them and their parents with problems affecting the rearing of children, regardless of auspices or setting.

The standards are directed to all who are concerned with improvement of services to children; to the general public, citizen groups, public officials, legislators, and the various professional groups; to those responsible for administration of services, board members and agency staff; to agencies whose functions include planning for and financing community services; to state departments entrusted by law with functions relating to licensing or supervision of organizations serving children; and to federations of agencies having requirements for membership that involve judgments on the nature of the organization and the kind of service rendered.

Standards can stimulate improvement of services only as they bring about dissatisfaction with present practices and conviction that change is desirable. They offer a base for examining and questioning practice and the premises from which it has been developed, and for evaluating the performance of child welfare agencies and the adequacy of existing services.

Standards are of use in planning, organization and administration of services; and in establishing state and local licensing requirements. They provide content for teaching and training in child welfare, in schools of social work, through inservice training and staff development programs, and in orientation of boards and volunteers. They can help to explain and justify expenditures, budget requests to federated fund-raising bodies and appropriation requests to legislatures. Finally, standards can promote understanding of how each service may more effectively meet needs of children, what it should be expected to do, and how it can be used. In that way, standards can help to gain greater public interest, understanding and support for adequate services, legislation and financing.

The Child Welfare League of America will undertake to review all the statements of standards at appropriate times. No standards of practice can be considered final; in one sense, the moment they are issued, they are out of date. Standards must be subject to continuous review and revision, in view of the constantly growing knowledge about children, human behavior and the treatment of human ills. Developments in the social and medical sciences, the evaluation of the effectiveness of current social work practices, policies and programs, and shifting patterns of social values and social organization should be conducive to change in child welfare practice.

Joseph H. Reid
Executive Director

December 1971

Standards for Services for Unmarried Parents

INTRODUCTION

Assistance for the problems associated with bearing and rearing children outside of marriage requires a complex framework of health care, education, welfare and legal resources in the community and the skills of various professional fields. These standards* apply to *services for unmarried parents,* provided through organized social agencies and supported by voluntary contributions and allocation of tax funds. Inherent in a social welfare service is a responsibility to use, coordinate and stimulate the development of the necessary resources available through other social institutions and individuals, so that they may be of optimum benefit to those in need of help.

These standards are based on current knowledge and experience in social work and related professional and scientific fields, and represent practices that are now considered to be the *best practices* in providing service for children born outside of marriage and for their parents, in a way that promotes their well-being.

Need for Specialized Services

Many of the significant services needed by unmarried parents are among the general community services for families and children. The variety and distinctive aspects of their problems warrant provision of differentiated services for unmarried parents. Moreover, it should be recognized that special skills are needed and have been developed to help unmarried parents with the problems they face as individuals and as parents. Such services should be available and identifiable as such, regardless of their agency setting or auspices.

*The first paragraph of each numbered section, however it is printed, represents the indicated standard. The rest of each section may be elaboration, explanation or illustration. Numbers in parentheses are cross-references to other sections in the statement.

1

0.1 Nature of the problem

Problems of parenthood outside of marriage have distinctive aspects that must be taken into consideration in order to provide adequate services.

Pregnancy and births out of wedlock occur in all societies. Where there is a definition of a socially approved family relationship, there will be births outside the definition. With the family at the base of our social structure, full equality of the child who is born in a marriage and one who is not will not come to pass.

Social and legal controls as well as community attitudes toward out-of-wedlock pregnancy and birth vary in place and in time by degree of sanction and of consequence for the individuals concerned.

Societal constraints that apply to the out-of-wedlock child and the unmarried parents have limited the opportunity for the individuals concerned to obtain access to all of the rights afforded their counterparts in legal marriage. New statutes and case law have modified some of the discriminations, but many still exist, rooted in common law and social mores.

In most communities, the child born out of wedlock lacks the right to his father's name and to his patrimony. Even when the father has acknowledged paternity or there has been a legal adjudication, the child's relationship to his father is generally limited.

The unmarried father, even when ascertained, may or may not have the right to custody and visitation or the right to be a legal parent, dependent upon the state, legal precedent and statutes that govern his rights. Thus the mother is frequently in the legal position of being the only parent. She may be denied school attendance, employment opportunities, public housing or public assistance.

The female-headed family should not necessarily be viewed as a deviant pattern of family life. It is more helpful to regard it as one type of family organization, and to consider what supports and services should be provided.

Specialized services for unmarried parents during pregnancy, childbirth and the child's infancy are only part of a spectrum of services that unmarried parents may need. The full range of maternal and child health services, supporting social and protective services, counseling and legal services is important to the well-being of children born out of wedlock and of their parents.

0.2 Extent of the problem

Public concern about the rise in the number of unmarried parents in this country is increasing. Many children are born to mothers who receive inappropriate or no prenatal care and get no help in planning for themselves and their children.

Some of the children will be brought up in fatherless families. Some move into two-parent families in legal adoption, a solution available predominantly to the child of the white unmarried mother.

Insufficient adoption opportunities for nonwhite children and the existence of unprotected adoptions, as well as the fact that many children born out of wedlock remain in poorly planned, long-term foster care, continue to be matters of concern.

Some unmarried parents are ill prepared emotionally, educationally and economically to carry effective parental roles. A significant sector of this group are victims of the unequal distribution of income and social services and medical care. In some circumstances, the persistence of poverty and hunger is of greater concern than child-rearing responsibilities.

Pregnant schoolgirls, especially the nonwhite and the poor, represent high-risk individuals. They constitute a critical social concern. Pregnancy out of wedlock during adolescence often requires a variety of services regardless of the plan for the child. Changing standards of sexual behavior and pregnancy at earlier ages cause concern to many in our society. The very young clearly need care and protection; the older adolescents need education and counseling, and their parents need help too.

0.3 Number and rate of out-of-wedlock births*

In recent years the rate of out-of-wedlock births rose very little, while the number of unmarried women of childbearing age increased considerably. The increase in the number of out-of-wedlock births was caused principally by an increased number of unmarried women. The increased need for social services and health care calls for a reexamination of the current pattern of community services in order to ensure better coordination and planning for services for unmarried parents.

0.4 Distribution by age†

The rate of out-of-wedlock births has been highest for women between the ages of 20 and 29 years old from 1940-1968; however, this age group's rate has declined in recent years. The rate for unmarried mothers under 20 years of age has continued to increase steadily. In 1968 slightly more than one-fifth of all unmarried mothers were girls of school age. Many of these school-age mothers may require child welfare services themselves and the care that the community affords to all children.

---

*The estimated number of illegitimate births in 1968 was 339,200. This represents nearly 10% of the total number of births in that year. The rate of out-of-wedlock births rose very little in the last 10 years, from 21.2 live births per thousand in 1958 to 23.4 births per thousand. (Source: National Center for Health Statistics, Health Services and Mental Health Administration, Public Health Service, Department of Health, Education and Welfare, Rockville, Maryland 20852—1971 Report.)

†National Center for Health Statistics—1971 Report.

0.5 Patterns and solutions to problems accompanying pregnancy out of wedlock

Patterns of behavior, from the motivation for involvement with the putative father to the arrangements for birth and plans for the child, vary with social class, and consequently selective social work services related to particular individuals and groups are required. The incidence of out-of-wedlock birth is estimated to be higher in the lower socioeconomic groups, in part because of differential access to family life education, knowledge and use of contraception, differential use of abortion and timing of marriage. Other factors are related to cultural variation in mating and marital patterns. Adolescent girls, both in terms of dating patterns and involvement with the father, provide a separate subgroup of unmarried parents. Moreover, the problems among the lower socioeconomic group require not only specialized social services, but broad community supports to alleviate poverty and preexisting difficulties.

0.6 Prevention

Many couples engage in premarital sexual relations. An unknown proportion of these avoid having children—either through contraception or abortion or because they are not fertile. Others get married after a premartial pregnancy, but before a premarital birth. Why some couples have children illegitimately and others do not awaits rigorous longitudinal studies to unravel more adequately the factors associated with births out of wedlock.

Prevention of the first birth is a most difficult and uncertain task. Prevention of subsequent births, however, through the provision of specialized services and full and adequate supportive community services for the unmarried parents and for their children may well be possible.

Assumptions Underlying Practice

0.7 Basic assumptions

Social services to unmarried parents are based upon certain assumptions and convictions:

Illegitimacy creates a social problem that has multiple causes and social, legal, moral and economic implications. The community has a responsibility to prevent the problems that it engenders and to identify and overcome the conditions giving rise to it, such as low social and economic status, inequality of opportunity, conflicting moral standards, devaluation of family life, personality disorders, ignorance or lack of preparation for marriage and family life.

Multiple health, education, welfare and other professional services are required to meet the needs of unmarried parents and their children, and should be coordinated for their benefit.

4

Society is responsible for the well-being of all of its members. It is of particular concern that each child should receive the care and protection he must have, and that his parents should have help if they need it to fulfill their child-rearing role or to recognize when they are incapable of doing so.

In order to strengthen family life, to prevent problems that may occur, and to make known the availability of its services, the community has a particular responsibility to reach out to those who may not come for help.

Social services for unmarried parents must be concerned with them as individuals and not only with planning for the child. The welfare of the child is, however, a primary consideration.

The child who remains with the unmarried mother has a right to have the interest of both parents and to know the father when this is in the child's best interest. The responsibility of an unmarried father extends beyond the obligation of financial support.

The rights of the parents and of the child must be respected and protected. If conflict exists between the rights of the child and of the parents, the best interest of the child is paramount.

1

SERVICES FOR UNMARRIED PARENTS AS A SOCIAL WELFARE FUNCTION

Services to unmarried parents are specialized social welfare services that express the concern of the community for the welfare of unmarried parents and of children born out of wedlock and that make available to them the help and protection they need and the resources necessary for their care.

1.1 Purpose

The purpose of services for unmarried parents should be

- to assure protection of the well-being and the rights of the child born out of wedlock and the well-being and the rights of the parents
- to make sure that their current needs are met
- to help them foresee and cope with consequent problems for the parent, child and community
- to help them achieve a satisfying and effective way of life
- to promote normal growth and development of the child

1.2 Individuals for whom services are appropriate

Services for unmarried parents should be available regardless of race, religion, ethnic group, legal residence, economic status, other children born out of wedlook or marital status. These services should be offered to the following:

- an expectant unmarried woman
- an unmarried mother who needs help with problems of new parenthood or planning for her own future or the child's well-being
- a formerly married woman who has given birth to a child but is not presently married to the father of this child
- a married woman whose husband is not the father of the child, and to her husband
- a woman who has conceived a child prior to her marriage
- the child born under any of these circumstances

6

- the natural father of a child born out of wedlock, irrespective of his legal relationship to the child and/or his marriage to someone other than the mother of his child

    In general the mother's need for services is different from the father's because of the physical and psychological aspects of pregnancy and the legal responsibilities that she carries for the child. Social agency services for unmarried parents have been geared primarily to meeting the needs of the mother and her child. However, these services should be extended to the father as well. (3.22–3.25)

1.3   Total service needed by unmarried parents

A total service for unmarried parents should include specialized services and the selective use and coordination of other community health, education and welfare resources to meet individual needs and to help with concerns associated with out-of-wedlock pregnancy and birth. (5.12)

    It should provide for the following:
    Reaching the unmarried mother and father. It is necessary to make known the services and resources available for the unmarried parents, both for themselves and the child. (2.1–2.6)

    Social work practice with the unmarried mother and father. Not every unmarried parent and child will need all the services that should be available in the community. It is the social worker's responsibility to help them use services selectively according to their needs in a coordinated manner, in ways that help them utilize their own potential resources and promote optimum social functioning. (3.1-2, 3.4-18, 3.21)

    Care of the child. Planning for the care of the child should take into consideration alternative plans based on the needs of the child and the mother, such as adoption, temporary foster family care, or care in the child's own home. (3.10–3.19)

    Medical care. Gynecological and obstetrical service during pregnancy, at the time of birth, and during the postpartum period should be available. Regular pediatric care and supervision of the child, plus special treatment for the health problems and physical handicaps of the mother and family planning services, should also be available. (4.1–4.22)

    Family life education. For potential or actual unmarried parents, especially adolescents who find themselves faced with new roles, education and counseling in family life should be available, and should include sex education, family planning, abortion, budgeting and financial planning, nutritional needs, and domestic arts. (8.8)

    Legal services. Legal advice and counseling should be available to the unmarried mother regarding the consequences of her decision to keep or to give up her child, and to both unmarried parents regarding the legal rights of the mother, the father and the child. (5.7)

Use of related resources. The unmarried parent should be helped to use any of the following resources, diagnostically selected on the basis of individual need:

- medical care (5.5—5.7)
- hospitalization (4.6, 4.11—4.21)
- financial assistance (5.14)
- living arrangements (6.1—6.29)
- legal services (5.8, 3.10)
- family planning (4.9, 5.18)
- education (5.11, 5.14, 8.8)
- vocational counseling (5.15)
- day care (5.16)
- psychiatric and psychological services (5.6, 5.8)
- religious counseling (5.9)
- recreation or socializing services (5.19)

1.4 Responsibility of social agency

The social agency should work cooperatively with other organizations and disciplines to make a comprehensive service available for all unmarried parents whose needs would otherwise be inadequately met. (5.13)

Insofar as possible, social services should be provided in a way that facilitates a continuing relationship, to make possible coordination of necessary resources and services and to ensure commitment to the mother and father in helping them carry out their plans.

The social agency has access to and is able to integrate the multiple social work, medical, legal, educational and other resources required to serve the unmarried parent. It has professionally trained and experienced staff with the skills to offer help based on individual and family needs.

2

REACHING THE UNMARRIED PARENT

Provisions to inform both the unmarried mother and father about available services should be an essential component of services for unmarried parents.

Studies and experience show that the prenatal and the postpartum periods can be a time of physical, social and psychological risk. Many unmarried mothers are in need of health care and both the unmarried father and mother should be encouraged to use social services to prepare for the necessary tasks and responsibilities associated with pregnancy and parenthood out of wedlock.

2.1 Need for special measures for reaching out to the unmarried parent

An aggressive program to reach the unmarried parents as early in the pregnancy as possible should be carried on to prevent unnecessary problems for them and the child and to make known the availability of skilled professional service to help in planning for the unmarried parents and the child.

Some unmarried mothers are not known to any professional service until the child's birth. Their needs may be urgent and may require immediate care to protect and assist mother and child.

Reluctance and hesitancy in seeking help are strongly intensified by the unmarried parents' expectation of disapproval or fears of investigation. This reluctance must be dealt with or it will tend to dilute the effectiveness of social services designed to facilitate the well-being of children born outside of marriage and their parents.

With the recognition that some groups, such as youths, the poor and the nonwhites, have difficulty in using social work services, especially designed measures to meet the common and unique needs of the several different groups are desirable. No one method or technique is applicable to all persons or effective for such varied groups of individuals. Most important is concern with the social problems that are frequently associated with pregnancy and birth outside of marriage, and effective resolution of these problems.

Because of the continuous demand for adoptable white infants, there are many people in the community who are ready to offer assistance to the unmarried mother for personal gain, to obtain the child for themselves or for other interested persons. Intervention by such people, even when they are well-meaning, presents hazards to many children, unmarried mothers, and adoptive families. In accepting such help, the unmarried mother may make plans inimical to the best interest of the child or herself and may fail to avail herself of professional service that can benefit her, the child and the adoptive parents.

2.2 Purpose of reaching out

Both the unmarried mother and father should be informed about available services so that

- they may use services of a qualified agency to consider plans for the care of the child
- they may use social services for an exploration of alternatives concerning plans for themselves individually or jointly
- the mother may have adequate health care, educational opportunities and social services
- the mother need not, out of panic or poor advice, estrange herself from her family, endanger her own health or safety or that of her child, or make a drastic change in employment, education or other areas of her life
- the father may clarify his own needs and concerns, especially those influenced by actual or prospective fatherhood
- the father may consider the means by which he can be helpful to the mother during and after pregnancy and in care of the child.

2.3 Conditions that make it possible to reach the unmarried parents

Services should be offered under conditions that encourage their use by unmarried parents, and contribute to their ease and security in using them.

It is not sufficient to inform the unmarried parents and referral sources about available services. Information and interpretation of available services should be a continuing process. The well-being and best interest of the parents and child are best served when the parents are helped to use legitimate community resources.

Health, education and social services should be available to all unmarried mothers, regardless of race, creed, color, legal residence, economic status, previous marital status or previous pregnancies. Restrictive eligibility requirements only serve to intensify existing personal and social problems.

The unmarried mother should not be required to relinquish her child, communicate with her family, prosecute the child's father, or accept a specific kind of religious teaching in order to be eligible for services.

Where the needs of the unmarried parents may be better met by another agency, information about the services available should be given, so that a choice can be considered. The service should not be punitive in nature, but should focus on the welfare of the mother and child and when indicated, on the unmarried father.

Pregnancy out of wedlock should not be made a reason for referral to the state training school for girls or to the state reformatory. Appropriate health, education and social welfare services should be made available, however, to pregnant girls and women who are in state training schools or other state institutions.

Services for unmarried parents should carry the assurance that a desire for privacy and confidentiality will be respected.

Minors who choose to exclude their parents should have the opportunity to use the social services for which parental consent is not legally required. Considerable skill and support may be necessary to modify the reluctance of a girl to tell her parents, and to win her cooperation in obtaining the consent necessary for care. (8.10)

In the event that the minor is emancipated, consideration should be given to recognition of the independent status.

2.4 Initiation of service by the agency

Agency service should be available not only for unmarried parents who can request help, but for those who are uncertain about using it. It should be offered to unmarried parents in the community who are recognized by others as needing help but who are unable to take the initiative to seek it.

In reaching out, the social agency makes its service known to the potential parents, their families and the community, and is ready to help them to use it if they choose to do so. Some unmarried parents have not had the experience of using social services, do not know how they can use community resources and social services, or may not believe that anyone is interested in helping them. Others will not come for service because of dependency, apathy, depression, helplessness, antisocial rebelliousness, or their judgment of their problems.

The practice of reaching out to those who need help calls for skill, imagination, creativity and a deep conviction about the service that can be given to the parents and an equally deep conviction about the right of the parents to accept or reject the service offered. The minor unmarried mother or the child of a mentally deficient or psychotic mother may require special protection, which a social agency can offer.

In some communities public schools, health facilities, hospitals and social agencies have developed coordinated systems of service to make available on a voluntary basis necessary care for pregnant women and unmarried mothers known to them. This arrangement provides an opportunity to offer social services to many who may need them who otherwise might be unknown and unreached.

Areas in which relatively larger numbers of unmarried mothers are located—by neighborhood, by community, institution or program of services—are effective and efficient sites of operations for social agencies to locate units of service such as information and referral, initial interview, or direct service.

Reporting out-of-wedlock pregnancies and births to the state welfare department so that each unmarried mother may be offered social services and informed of the resources available to her is compulsory in a few states. It should be noted, however, that this statute is most effective as part of a system of reaching-out practices in which the provision of services is adequate to the needs.

Social agencies need to be prepared for more applicants whenever greater efforts to bring unmarried parents into service are made.

2.5 The use of mass media

Social agencies should use the mass media (television, radio and the press) and other community institutions to offer information about services for unmarried parents.

Lack of information about community resources should not be a reason for unmarried parents to take a course of action inimical to their welfare or that of the child.

Because agencies are concerned with social problems they should utilize the local communication networks to educate the community about the complex nature of out-of-wedlock pregnancy and birth and to gain community support for these services and for programs to attack the social problems associated with out-of-wedlock pregnancy and birth. (8.4)

2.6 Interpretation to key groups in the community

Social agencies should inform the key groups in the community that are sources of referral about their services, through direct contact and through use of interpretive material, such as brochures, films and leaflets describing available resources and programs.

Interpretation and information should be directed to groups of young men and women who are or may become users of service.

It is particularly important to work closely with school authorities in the interpretation of agency services, since the situations coming to their attention are often those of the youngest unmarried mothers, who may require child welfare services and protective care in addition to help with the problems of out-of-wedlock pregnancy and childbirth.

The medical profession and other allied health professions and personnel are the initial groups in the community to which the unmarried mother is likely to turn for help. Doctors, nurses, public health workers and members of hospital staffs frequently see the mother at an early stage in her pregnancy or near the time of delivery. Their understanding and acceptance of the need for special services are indispensable if they are to help her make good use of community resources.

Informative material should be prepared for the medical profession and other health professions and distributed to the medical societies, hospital councils and professional associations.

In addition, interpretation should be carried on to the fullest extent possible between the social agency, the physician and the hospital.

Among the key groups to which unmarried mothers may turn for help are clergymen, lawyers, individual teachers and school counselors, as well as school social workers and principals. Some of the other groups include druggists, personnel directors and labor union counselors. Interpretation should be carried on with such groups and informative materials distributed, so that they also may make appropriate referrals.

3

SOCIAL WORK WITH UNMARRIED PARENTS

The provision of social services for unmarried parents and their families carries with it a responsibility to help them cope with a variety of factors associated with pregnancy and parenthood outside of marriage. The unmarried mother and her family are often seen for continued service; the father should be included.

Social work responsibility may be shared by the social workers in a hospital or health department, in a maternity home or in another social agency that provides other services for the unmarried parent. Social work responsibility may also be a part of the service provided by other professional groups such as educators and medical personnel.

Social work includes individual and group counseling and community activities that prevent and forestall some of the common and specific problems associated with pregnancy and parenthood outside of marriage.

Social Work with the Unmarried Parents

Social work with unmarried parents must be concerned with them as individuals and with planning for their children. Family members of the unmarried parents may also require social services to cope with the pregnancy and birth out of wedlock.

3.1 Social work goals

With increasing recognition of the personal and legal problems, social, economic and psychological risks, as well as health hazards associated with unmarried pregnancy and childbirth, social work should be directed to the following goals:

- the prevention of impediments to the future of the child's life and opportunities, as well as the prevention of impediments to the future adjustment of the unmarried parents for realization of their best interests
- the promotion of the unmarried parents' abilities and the enhancement of their capacities for more satisfying and effective lives as a result of supportive rela-

14

tionships with the social worker and the self-awareness that can be gained through social work services

- designing and deciding on plans that are in the best interest of the child and parents
- the maximal use of personal family and community resources to effect plans that are best for themselves and for their children.

3.2 Use of social work

Social work should be provided to assist the unmarried parent during pregnancy and confinement and until the special needs arising from the unmarried pregnancy and birth have been met with a plan that assures the child's future protection.

The unmarried parents may need help and encouragement in

- finding and using community resources to meet immediate and individual needs such as health care, housing, financial assistance, legal services, schooling and employment
- dealing with the specific physical, social, emotional and spiritual problems and stresses arising from pregnancy and birth of a child outside of marriage
- gaining understanding about preexisting problems that may have some bearing on the pregnancy or that complicate the situation
- reaching and carrying out a decision about a suitable plan for the child
- obtaining resources and services needed for the child
- planning for the future with or without the child, with or without each other
- forming meaningful and growth-producing interpersonal relationships with their families, peers and other persons.

Some unmarried parents may require and want help only in utilizing available resources; others require continued social services, especially if they are themselves children or if the child's welfare may be jeopardized.

Social work with the unmarried parents and their families must be provided according to the individual needs, problems, motivation and capacity. This involves

- an understanding of the situation, including present realities and life experiences that have a bearing upon the situation
- an identification of (1) the capacities and strengths of the mother to meet the tasks and responsibilities of her pregnancy or out-of-wedlock child, with due regard for her rights and problems; (2) the capacities and strengths of the father to meet the responsibilities of his relationship with the unmarried mother and with the child; (3) the factors in the mother's and father's environment that help or hinder them in meeting present responsibilities; (4) problems of each that may be anticipated prior to and following the birth of the child

- assistance in the formulation of a plan for a course of action to cope with the needs and the problems of the parent and child, which can be carried out in the context of the resources and realities of the situation
- assisting the unmarried parents to carry out the chosen plan.

To meet the varying needs of each individual, the social worker must utilize and coordinate selectively resources and services in the community in addition to those that the agency provides directly.

3.3 Social work methods

Social work methods, including casework, group work and community organization, should be selected according to the needs of the individual unmarried parents and in relation to their purpose in seeking help.

A casework relationship should be used to help the individual unmarried parents to focus on individual problems, to cope with the personal meaning of their concern, to consider the choices that can be helpful to them, and to develop productive ways of using themselves and their circumstances.

The use of group work differs from the individual relationship in that members of the group are enabled to help each other. Groups provide a setting in which leadership, organized contact and peer group interaction can be used. The purpose of groups should be clearly defined in order to determine the structure that best suits the purpose of the group, as well as the role of the group leader.

Groups have been used for

- education, orientation and information
- group counseling and emotional support
- group psychotherapy.

Community organization involves a variety of interventive strategies that the unmarried parent may need and want. It serves as a significant vehicle for mobilizing and coordinating needed services and resources in the community for individual and specific groups of unmarried parents.

3.4 The initial contact

The initial contact should serve to

- demonstrate immediate concern for and interest in the unmarried mother or father and a readiness and competence to help them in some way
- obtain such information as is needed to understand the situation and the concern of the unmarried parent, and to evaluate together the need for service
- make clear to the unmarried parent what kind of help is available, how this service is given, and what the requirements are for using it

16

- appraise the capacity of the unmarried parents and, when appropriate, the families to use help
- arrive at a mutual understanding of whether a brief or continuing service is needed
- establish a base for continuing service.

3.5 Basis for service

The social worker should help the unmarried parents take part in discussing and understanding the problem and situation during the initial contact and thereafter, in a way that gives evidence of the kind of help that is offered and that facilitates a mutual basis for continuing service.

This involves explaining the nature of the service, the requirements for using it, such as frequency and place of interviews, the participants and the assignments of workers.

The experience of participating in the initial process should help the parents to understand what is required and what help they can expect to get.

3.6 Planning termination of service

The basis for termination of the service should be included in the initial plan. The social worker and the unmarried parents should set goals and agree on a period of time for evaluating the use of the service and the need for further service.

It is helpful to establish regular intervals for the purpose of shared evaluation and to set up a method by which the worker and the unmarried parent can discuss their evaluations and arrive at a basis for future planning.

The social worker has to evaluate continually the relationship with the parent and the care of the child. The social worker has to be close enough to the parent to understand the parent's responses, but detached enough to perceive and evaluate the responses appropriately and to respond appropriately. It is desirable for the social worker to review and record the experience with the unmarried parent in interview or group activity, and to use supervision or consultation for periodic evaluation.

Joint evaluation with cooperating agencies should also take place regularly.

3.7 Initial participation of family members

The number of interviews required and the determination of who needs to participate initially are determined by the evaluation of the situation for which help is needed. (3.27)

Generally, one or both of the unmarried parents will be expected to participate. The participation of other members of the family depends on their involvement with the unmarried parents. In some instances the unmarried

17

parents may need to establish a basis for service themselves, which may mitigate against family participation during the initiation of services with the unmarried parents.

At other times it may be important for the worker to see the family of youthful unmarried parents. Observations of the family and their responsiveness to the unmarried parents may be essential for the initial understanding of the situation.

A family's willingness to participate in the use of service needs to be respected, whether or not they are living with one of the unmarried parents.

Social Work Responsibility in Assisting the Unmarried Parents

The social worker should help the unmarried parents clarify plans they can make that will be helpful to them in their decision about pregnancy and birth out of wedlock.

3.8 Premarital counseling

Counseling for the unmarried mother and father who are considering marriage, especially the teenage parent, should be an essential element of the service.

Despite the significance and duration of premarital relationships in many instances, premarital pregnancy may impose emotional and realistic strains on a marriage; exploration of the meaning and the expectations of marriage to the prospective marital partners are significant aspects of premarital counseling.

If the unmarried parent is a minor, parental consent is generally required. It is thus often necessary for the family to be involved with the expectant parents to determine whether marriage is in the best interest of the unmarried parents and the child.

3.9 Termination of Pregnancy

Since some issues cannot be validated by knowledge and are a matter of opinion and conviction, and since termination of pregnancy is one such issue, the Child Welfare League of America is not taking a stand either favoring or opposing abortion or the question of whether it should be legalized.

Counseling services and referral to a qualified medical resource, when indicated, should be available to unmarried pregnant girls and women who wish to consider the alternative of abortion. (4.5)

A legal abortion is possible in some states and thus is a possibility that some individuals may wish to consider. An illegal abortion continues to be hazardous to the health of the mother.

18

Counseling should help the expectant mother to express any fears and anxieties about an abortion and the meaning the pregnancy has for her. If she should decide on abortion, social services should continue as indicated, including counseling services following the abortion.

The unmarried pregnant girl or woman may need to consider her own religious, ethical and moral convictions about abortion. Counseling should assist her to do so and to make an individual decision that is right for her.

In some circumstances, particularly among minor unmarried pregnant girls, these deliberations will involve the unmarried father and the families of unmarried parents. The feelings of the unmarried father and of family members often are a decisive factor in decisions and plans to abort or to complete pregnancy. The unmarried pregnant girl or woman should be encouraged to use their help when it is available, to arrive at a decision that is best for her.

A significant sector of society rejects abortion and holds that it is an objectionable practice. There is the conviction that an unborn child has the right to birth. Social agencies, individual staff members, and unmarried parents who object to abortion should not be expected to participate in discussion or counseling about abortion. Social agencies should make known their policies and procedures with respect to abortion, just as they do with other services they offer.

Social Work Responsibility in Planning for the Child

The social worker should help the unmarried parents to clarify their parental rights and responsibilities and to make an acceptable plan for the child.

3.10 Parental rights and responsibilities

The social worker should assist the unmarried parents to secure clarification of their legal rights and responsibilities for the child, so that each may know and exercise these rights and responsibilities. Such clarification helps the parents in their planning for the child and for themselves. (5.7)

Within the United States, the unmarried mother generally has sole rights to custody of her child, and the reciprocal obligation to provide for his support, care and general welfare, with such help as society can give.

The unmarried father has no legal right to the custody of his child. Generally he has only a moral obligation to support his child unless this obligation has been made legal by formal acknowledgment of paternity, or by legal adjudication of paternity through court action. In such cases, in many states the father does not acquire the legal status of a parent and his consent to wardship or adoption is not required. However, if adoption is planned, an agency should safeguard the child and itself against future litigation by obtaining consent, waiver or disclaimer wherever possible, even in cases where the admission of paternity has been only informal.

In our culture the rights of the parents must be exercised for the child's benefit; otherwise they must yield to the child's interest and welfare. A parent may not divest himself of parental responsibilities, except through process of law and with full protection of the child.

Termination of the mother's rights to her child should take place only through voluntary relinquishment to an authorized agency, when provided for by statute, or through legal procedures that terminate parental rights and transfer responsibility for the child to an agency authorized by law to assume the powers and duties of legal custody and the right to consent to an adoption. (3.19)

If the mother is a minor, additional legal safeguards may be required, such as the requirement of consent for adoption from her parents or guardian, or for appointment of a guardian *ad litem.* (8.10)

If the mother has a legal husband, there is a legal presumption of paternity on his part, even though he may not be the father of the child. Therefore, unless his nonpaternity has been judicially established, his consent to adoption or relinquishment of paternal rights is required. If the legal husband refuses to involve himself in any legal procedure and has no real interest in the child, the situation should be brought to court for legal review.

3.11 Help in planning for the child

The unmarried mother should have counseling services to reach a decision without delay that will be best for her and for the child, and support in carrying it through.

The unmarried mother generally has the right to determine her plan for the child and may need help to understand her motives, the reality of preparing for a child, and the resources available to her.

The father should have assistance with his feelings and desires about the plan for the child, his concerns about the legal implications, and his legal and moral responsibilities for the child.

The social worker has the responsibility to discuss with unmarried parents the various solutions available and to face realistically with the mother the meaning of her decision for herself and for her child. In addition, by conscious use of the professional relationship, the social worker can help the unmarried parents to cope with and work through many of their personal concerns and to consider the reality aspects of the situation, with an emphasis on the current and long-range implications for the child's care and for their own lives.

In helping them make a plan for the child, it is necessary to take into consideration the meaning of the child to them, the relationship between the mother and father, their relationship with their own families, the personal strengths and environmental opportunities to meet their needs and those of the child, as well as consideration of what resources are necessary.

There is no one plan that offers an ideal solution for all children born out of wedlock. This is perhaps the biggest issue the parents face, and it frequently causes much conflict in reaching a decision.

Despite the negative views of some persons about out-of-wedlock births, the increasing acceptance of single-parent families often influences the mother's decision. There are however, long-term implications and responsibilities that must be considered for their advantages as well as any disadvantages in the planning for the child.

In the majority of cases, the mother keeps her child. The mother should, however, have every opportunity to consider as alternatives adoption or placement in temporary foster family care. No consideration of optimal choices is viable unless true alternatives exist: many mothers, aware of the lack of real choice, may select a plan that seems possible rather than one that has the optimal advantage for her child and herself.

If it is determined on the basis of a professional appraisal that the mother is not meeting the child's needs, the agency should act protectively in behalf of the child and take action to terminate parental rights. In some instances the father may be a potential resource for the care and custody of the child, if the mother's parental rights are terminated. His interest should be clearly, preferably legally, established; he should also have a suitable plan that is in the best interest of the child.

The permanent or current incapacity of some mothers to fill the role of parents or meet the needs of the child must be faced, and alternatives considered and provided for the care of the infant. In special situations where the child is physically handicapped, the agency should assist the mother to utilize the necessary health resources, or the agency should accept surrender when the mother desires to relinquish the child. Community resources should be utilized and integrated for the child's care.

In situations where the mother is not responsible because she is mentally deficient or mentally ill or a child herself, a protective function may have to be exercised in behalf of the child. The legal status of a minor unmarried mother or age alone should not be the primary factor in this consideration.

Keeping the Child

3.12 Decision to keep the child

If the mother wishes to consider keeping her child, the social worker should help her to consider her strengths and the various aspects of her situation, including the resources in her family and the community, and thus help her determine whether she can provide for the child.

In helping the mother to consider keeping her child, the following should be kept in mind:

- The mother should be helped to assess carefully the many related problems she will face if she rears her child. The mother should be offered continuing social work help, particularly during the first year of the child's birth, and the opportunity to make another plan for herself and the child if she finds that her first plan is not in her best interests or in the interest of her child. The child's father may be an important part of this decision making if he offers emotional and financial support to the mother and child.

- The schoolage mother who plans to return to her parental home with her child must consider the makeup of her family, their ability to accept her and the baby, their respect for her role as the child's mother and their readiness to help her to meet her responsibilities. The willingness of the family and the availability of community resources for the provision of social resources — for example, care for the child and career preparation for the mother — must be considered.

- The older unmarried mother who has or plans to set up an independent household for herself and her child also faces a variety of needs. Her experience differs from that of the widow or divorcee with a child, in that they have had at least an image of a family and possibly the experience of a family at one point. It must be remembered, however, that this independent household is sometimes a temporary arrangement that may be followed by marriage and a two-parent family life.

Realistic factors governing the setting up of an independent household would be the mother's financial needs, decisions about continued schooling, working and supporting a child, the effect of this kind of existence upon her capacity to provide a warm, happy life for her child and a rewarding life for herself. Whether she plans to work, attend school or remain at home, a certain portion of usual family life may be denied to her, for she does not have a husband to share the parental and family responsibility.

The social worker should refer the mother for financial assistance (5.13) if she needs it or give some assistance directly if the agency policy so provides. Assistance to the mother to make living arrangements for herself and her child and to utilize medical and other health care, as well as other community facilities, may be required.

3.13 Keeping the child in own home

If it is determined that the mother is able to give the care, guidance and supervision a child needs, she should have all possible assistance, from all resources in the community, to carry out a sound plan to keep her child. (5.13 – 5.19)

To serve the best interest of the child and the parent, it is important to understand the interplay of such factors as the relationship of the mother and father, their attitudes about marriage and child rearing, the level of financial adequacy and economic security, as well as their social expectations and self-confidence. Within this frame of reference the social worker should direct attention to the following:

- Changes in personal and family relationships and roles frequently require realignments of a sensitive nature, particularly among adolescents and young adults. Mothers who rear their children have a new set of responsibilities that may require new learning and some changes in their lives. The measure of adequacy in meeting basic needs is of major significance in the success of the mother's planning. Often realities such as housing, finances, health care and child care are concerns that must be dealt with.

- Increasing evidence of the importance and duration of the relationships between the unmarried parents should alert the social worker to the necessity of assisting them to develop a viable relationship with the child that does not obstruct their individual interests or their well-being. Some unmarried couples are not legally free to marry one another and may need help to effect desired marital plans. Community resources such as legal services, free or at cost, should be considered. Others, unready for marriage to each other, seek other relationships that in some instances result in a later marriage; a number of unmarried mothers are involved primarily in family relationships with their own parents. Care must be taken to assess the individual situation for appropriate approaches in the best interest of the child and the parents, with due consideration for any cultural elements that influence individual planning.

- A significant number of fathers are interested in contributing to the support of their children. Such assumptions of responsibility should be encouraged as one aspect of the father's interest in the well-being of his child. Other integral features of fatherhood such as visiting the child and legitimating the child should be determined with the best interest of the child in mind.

- Adequate career preparation and financial sufficiency are important components of success for the unmarried parent who keeps her child. Unless it is contraindicated by individual circumstance, the unmarried mother should have the opportunity to develop her potential concurrent with the responsibilities of parenthood. This may include continued education, vocational counseling and job training, as well as assistance with employment opportunities and housing. Adequate child care is a significant part of such planning and should include consideration of the resources within the family and in the community.

- The younger mothers usually know little about the physical, mental or emotional aspects of childrearing. Because these young women themselves need much support, they may require extended periods of support by an agency, the family and community resources to enable them to gain the skills and understanding necessary for their well-being and the provision of child care. Most often, the very young mothers who keep their children should be part of families that help them with the responsibilities of childrearing, and help the mothers to use the services and resources available to them.

23

Individual and group services focused on child care and family life education are often helpful to the unmarried mother.

3.14 The use of foster family care*

Foster family care should be used selectively as a valuable resource for interim care of the child for whom a permanent plan cannot be made immediately, but its indefinite prolongation should be avoided wherever possible. Residential group care of infants and children under 6 years old in institutions and hospitals is not acceptable practice.

Temporary care should be available for the child whose mother needs to work out plans for establishing a home with the child in the near future or for the child who is to be adopted.

Assurance of good foster family care for an interim period may prevent the mother who is uncertain from making a hasty decision that might be harmful to herself or the child.

Placement can be planfully used as a testing-out period for the mother who wants to keep her child, to help her become acquainted with her child, face her feelings for the child and the responsibility she will have to assume, such as financing the baby's care, acknowledging the child to her family and friends if she plans to make a home for herself and the child later, and direct care of the child.

Relinquishing the Child †

3.15 Early relinquishment

Sufficient social work help should be provided for the unmarried mother who is planning to relinquish her child for adoption so that she can make the decision about relinquishment as early as possible after the birth of the child. (5.7)

All procedures regarding relinquishment should be understood clearly by unmarried parents who consider adoption for the child.

Early relinquishment is advantageous for the infant in making permanent placement possible at an early age and for the mother in avoiding delay that may increase her concerns and her problems about her own life situation. Delay may result in her inability to relinquish the child even though this may be the best plan for them both.

---

*See CWLA Standards for Foster Family Care Service, 1959.

†For a full discussion of adoption services, see CWLA Standards for Adoption Service, revised 1968. The Standards that are essential for services for unmarried parents are included in this section.

3.16 Emotional readiness to relinquish

Relinquishment should be taken according to the mother's emotional readiness to give up the child, and not according to either the agency's ability to place the child or the immediate availability of a home.

It should not be a general requirement that the parents see or not see the child or bring the child to an adoption agency themselves. Nor should it be assumed the conflicts are minimized and relinquishment necessarily made easier when the parents do not see the child. The relinquishment of the child is usually a difficult experience for the mother and support to her during and following termination of parental rights is helpful.

3.17 Separation from the child

When adoption is the plan, the adoption service should be prepared to accept the child as soon as the mother and the agency decide that the mother is ready to relinquish the child.

3.18 Termination of parental rights

In the case of an unmarried mother who voluntarily relinquishes the child to an authorized agency, proper legal procedures for termination of parental rights should be established. When it has been determined that in all probability the unmarried mother will be unable to fulfill her responsibility to give the child the security of a permanent home, but is unable or unwilling to relinquish the child voluntarily, the agency should request the court to act in the interest of the child on involuntary termination (or deprivation) of parental rights. (8.14)

3.19 Protection of finality and legality of relinquishment

The relinquishment of a child should be accepted only when the unmarried mother has had an opportunity to make a decision that she believes is best for herself and the child, and that she recognizes to be final. This final step should not be taken until the unmarried mother is ready emotionally to give up her rights, as well as her responsibilities, to the child.

The use of informal relinquishment procedures, blind consents by the unmarried parent or any other procedure that has the result of postponing the time of permanent termination of parental rights until actual entry of an adoption decree is hazardous and fails to serve the interests of the parties to whom the child-placing agency has a major obligation.

3.20 Duration of parental responsibility

Parental responsibility should end when an authorized social agency accepts relinquishment of the child and parental rights are terminated.

Social Work With the Adolescent Mother

The adolescent often requires a variety of social services, which may include foster care or protective services. In the provision of social service, it is important to recognize the differences between helping the adolescent and helping the older and the more experienced person. The school-age unmarried parent has particular needs related to the status of pupil as well as the parental responsibility. In her own best interest the school girl may need to remain with a family (her own or a foster family) for the personal care and emotional support a family provides.

3.21 Understanding the personality of the adolescent

In work with the adolescent unmarried parent, the social worker should take into account personality characteristics and developmental stages that differentiate adolescents from each other and from older persons.

Typical stages of adolescence may be easily confused with deep emotional disturbances. Commonly adolescents are involved in a peer culture differing with adult values, striving for their own identity, uncertain and changeable. Withdrawal, apathy and sadness call for special attention to discern the depth and breadth of feeling in relation to the circumstances.

An out-of-wedlock pregnancy imposes new demands to meet the situation. It may intensify typical adolescent traits such as weakly fixed identity, rebellion, emotional instability and lack of trust. Adolescents may require special assistance for continued work on developmental growth phases.

It is important to keep in mind the developmental stages and problems of youth as they interrelate with sexual education and heterosexual relationships, pregnancy and parenthood. Many teenagers are inadequately prepared for the sexual expressiveness they evidence. They may need help to understand this themselves and to develop personal standards.

The adolescents may need special consideration in recognizing opportunities available to them, qualifying for them and persevering in spite of frustrations and rebuffs. Guilt or shame, fears of the future and of possible rejection may be major components of their concern.

Social Work With the Independent Unmarried Mother

The woman who has been independent and able to manage her own affairs, or who may be maintaining a home of her own, may not come to a social agency at the time of her pregnancy, or may need help only in making suitable living arrangements.

3.22 Special needs of the independent mother

Specialized services should be available for the independent unmarried mother who has kept her child and who may have other children born in or out of wedlock. For the best interest of the mother and child, it is important to help her plan for herself and her child to cope with the special problems she may have in the care and up-bringing of a child born out of wedlock.

The independent unmarried mother is not always one who is older chrono-logically. She may be young in years, but self-reliant or unable to live with her family. Primarily she differs from the dependent unmarried mother in that her social setting affords her a greater opportunity for self-determination and demands a greater degree of competence in handling the situation herself.

The fact of parenthood or birth of the child may represent a crisis to her. At such a time the social worker can help her with her concerns and help her to plan for her future and the future of the child.

The life of the independent mother suggests that she is able to manage her own affairs. Although she is already maintaining a home of her own, she may need a larger one. Often she is divorced or separated from her husband, and may have other legal complications surrounding the legitimation of the child. The situation is likely to be complicated by external social and economic forces that lessen opportunities for the optimal care of the child and herself. Special attention to the needs of the independent mother to assist her with these reality pressures can be of advantage to mother and child.

Social Work With the Unmarried Father

The unmarried father, especially the adolescent, should have an opportunity for social work help. Social agencies offering counseling services and family welfare services as well as specialized services for unmarried parents should reach out to the father more than they have in the past, and should specify services for unmarried fathers among those they offer.

The unmarried father is increasingly available and anxious to help in planning for his baby. His moral responsibility for the child as well as the legal responsibility of an acknowledged father, leads him in many cases to contri-bute to the care of the child and offer support to the mother. Often he can use help to determine the ways in which his ability, desire and plans to help with the child may become most effective. This focus involves the meaning unmarried parenthood has for him, and an assessment of his relationship to the mother.

3.23 Consideration of the father's individual needs and problems

In providing social work for the unmarried father, it is important to approach him as a prospective or actual parent and as an individual with his own needs and problems, rather than as an adjunct to the plan for the unmarried mother and child, or only as a source of financial support.

Relationships between the unmarried parents are often very meaningful, and should be one focus of attention in the services for unmarried parents.

Usually the mother is the most successful person in getting the father to come to the agency, although a direct approach to him by the social worker is often an effective means of reaching him. However, no mother should be denied service if she is unable to include the father or chooses to exclude him. The social worker should provide safeguards for his privacy similar to those offered to the mother.

Many unmarried fathers, particularly the younger men, need the opportunity to bring their real feelings about the situation into the open in order that they may understand more clearly their own involvement and their responsibility. The father may require some assistance with his feelings about the past and present relationship to the mother, as well as the concerns about the legal implications and his moral responsibility to the child. If the mother relinquishes custody of the child, the father may be a resource for the care of the child if he has established paternity and has a plan that is in the best interests of the child.

3.24 Decision to involve the father

The decision about whether to involve the father in planning for the unmarried mother and her child, and to what extent, should take into consideration the expressed wishes of the unmarried mother, what the father knows about the situation, and other factors.

The agency's knowledge that he is the alleged father of a child born out of wedlock is reason enough to offer him an interview. His response will depend in part upon the tone of the offer and the reason given for the agency's wish to talk with him.

The mother should understand how involving the father can be a positive step for both. In planning for the child, it is an acknowledgment that the child has two parents, both of whom are significant to his future.

Where indicated, the social worker should help the mother accept a plan for involving the unmarried father, and encourage her to get him to contact the same worker, or another worker, if necessary.

If the child is to be placed for adoption, the agency should know about both parents to make the best plan for him.

Direct knowledge of the father by the social worker has advantages for the child.

3.25 Use of legal proceedings

Wherever possible, social work rather than direct court action should be used to get the father to participate in planning and to accept financial responsibility.

Decision to take legal action should be based on a good social work plan and legal advice, and should not be made a requirement of financial assistance to the unmarried mother, nor a condition of planning for the child.

3.26 Responsibility for support

The unmarried father should have the opportunity to consider how much responsibility for the child he is willing and able to assume, and not just the responsibility to support him.

The purpose of legal action establishing paternity should be to legitimate the child and to secure his rights, including the right to the support of his father.

3.27 Social work with the family

Social work services should be offered to the family of the unmarried parent or to individual family members when such planning is beneficial for the unmarried parents and for the child.

The crisis situation, interpersonal conflict, and concern about changing family composition and role are some of the reasons that impel families to seek social work service. In addition, family members often desire to help the unmarried parent with the problems of out-of-wedlock pregnancy and birth.

In some circumstances, the impact of pregnancy or parenthood outside of marriage on specific family members, such as younger siblings and parents of the unmarried parents, may be acute. Special attention to their concern may prevent future problems for them and may be helpful in their relationship to the unmarried parent. The adolescent sisters and brothers of the unmarried parents are considered to be particularly vulnerable and may require specific attention to their needs.

Some families of the unmarried parents are very helpful to the unmarried parents by providing financial and emotional support as well as assistance in planning with them and for the child. The father as well as the mother of the unmarried parent has a significant role as a concerned person who can be helpful.

Recognition of the right of the unmarried parents to plan for the child and for themselves is important in working with the family, except when the unmarried parents are too young or immature to make decisions.

4

MEDICAL AND HOSPITAL SERVICES

Provision of medical service is essential for the well-being of the mother and child. It should be a protection by the community to prevent problems that may result if the health of the mother and the child is not adequately safeguarded.

The unmarried mother, like all other mothers, should have medical care that meets high standards regardless of her financial means, race, creed or legal residence.

4.1 Responsibility for meeting health needs

The social agency serving the unmarried mother should share responsibility with the agencies, obstetricians, gynecologists and other health professionals providing health care and medical services in reaching unmarried mothers, to see to it that all of their health needs are met. (2.2)

4.2 Integration of social work and medical services

Medical services should be integrated with overall planning and social work services for the unmarried mother and her baby, so that interchange and pertinent information can take place freely and both services can work harmoniously for the same ultimate goals. (5.4–5.6)

It should be a concern of the physician, social worker and other professional staff involved in medical care and other services to foster a mutual understanding of and respect for the contributions of each other.

4.3 Source of medical care

The agency should assist the unmarried mother to arrange for medical care by a private physician, preferably an obstetrician or pediatrician in his office, or by a physician employed by a clinic, hospital or maternity home.

The prospective mother should have a choice of medical resources insofar as this is possible and as long as the resources meet accepted standards of medical practice.

The unmarried mother who keeps her child should be assisted to use community resources that offer health services for her and for the child. These resources include pediatricians, obstetricians, maternal and infant care centers, health conferences and well-baby clinics, visiting nurses, public health workers, and the social service departments of hospitals and clinics.

Basic Requirements for Medical Care

4.4 Standards of medical care

Medical care should conform to the standards established by the American College of Obstetricians and Gynecologists* and the American Academy of Pediatrics.†

Prenatal care should be provided by a physician or duly licensed clinic.

Medical care and services to be provided for the unmarried mother and her child include

- prenatal care (4.5)
- abortion, if desired and legally available (4.5)
- hospitalization and nursing care at time of delivery (4.6)
- diagnosis and treatment of all medical problems (4.5)
- dental examination and treatment
- postpartum care of the mother (4.7)
- family planning (4.9)
- pediatric care of the baby (4.8)
- medical social work services (4.21)
- followup services
- allied health services, including nutritional guidance, nursing and health instruction.

Adequate medical care is based on the recognition of the interrelationship of physical, social, emotional and spiritual factors.

4.5 Prenatal care

Arrangements for periodic examinations during pregnancy should be made
- to predict the kind of delivery that must be planned for
- to instruct the mother in dietary needs and in care of herself during pregnancy

---

* Manual of Standards in Obstetric-Gynecologic Practice. The American College of Obstetricians and Gynecologists, March 1959, —Revised 1965. (79 West Monroe, Chicago 90, Ill.)
† Standards and Recommendations for Hospital Care of Newborn Infants. American Academy of Pediatrics, 1954. (1801 Hinman Ave., Evanston, Ill.)

- to diagnose and treat any health problems that are present or that may develop during the pregnancy
- to help prepare the expectant mother for developmental changes and the experience of childbirth.

If the unmarried expectant mother wishes a legal abortion, she should have the opportunity to discuss with the physician the medical procedures and implications. In the case of a minor, medical consent from a parent or guardian is usually required by law. No physician should be required to perform nor should any unmarried mother be forced to accept an abortion.

During the period of pregnancy the medical personnel who provide medical care to the prospective mother should help her to prepare for the delivery. This would include discussion of the anxieties and fears associated with childbirth, the nutritional needs of pregnancy, and an explanation of the physical aspects of pregnancy and birth. It should be recognized that during pregnancy or at the time of confinement, when dormant or repressed feelings may be activated, the unmarried mother has in addition to any other problems the same conflicts, fears and patterns of relating as other pregnant women. Special medical provisions by clinics and hospitals for young adolescents can be helpful.

The prospective mother should have opportunity to attend mothers' classes to learn how to care for herself and for the baby. This can help some to accept pregnancy and others to decide what they want to do about the baby, as they face the reality of what is involved in the care of a child.

4.6 Hospitalization at time of delivery

Confinement should take place in an accredited hospital meeting recognized standards, with facilities for dealing with complicated cases or emergencies, as well as seemingly routine cases.

Insofar as possible the mother should be helped to select for the delivery an accredited hospital (4.11)

- that makes provision for social services as part of total medical care or comprehensive service (4.21)
- in which the administration and staff have an interest in and understanding of the unmarried mother
- in which a financial arrangement can be worked out by the mother and the hospital. (4.13, 4.15)

4.7 Postpartum care of the mother

Provision should be made to ensure the mother's return after delivery to a clinic or private physician for medical care, instructions on diet, exercise, or any immediate treatment that may be indicated.

It should be the responsibility of the doctor and the social agency to inform the mother of her need for adequate postpartum care for her own sake and for the sake of the child.

Whenever possible the social worker should assist the mother to initiate arrangements for continued medical care, and the social agency should follow up if she does not return for postpartum care.

Public health agencies may carry responsibility for adequate followup of the mothers known to them.

4.8 Pediatric care of the baby

Suitable pediatric care should be provided for the baby after discharge from the hospital, whether the child is with his mother, in foster care or placed for adoption.

Medical services should be accessible and available to facilitate pediatric care for the child.

If the unmarried mother keeps her child with her, she should have instruction in methods of child care. Besides the private pediatrician or physician, various community resources such as maternity and infant care centers, child health conferences, well-baby clinics, and special programs of nursing services or an agency nurse may be used for this purpose.

Neonatal drug addiction is of increasing concern. Some infants of mothers who have abused drugs may need immediate observation or treatment to ensure health.

4.9 Family planning services

Provision should be made to assist all unmarried parents to obtain family planning services if they choose to use them. (5.17)

If an unmarried parent wishes information about family planning, the physician and other hospital or health personnel should be prepared to discuss methods of contraception with her.

It is the responsibility of the physician and the social worker to ensure that no mother is coerced into control of conception, but that accessible family planning services be available for all who choose to use them.

It should be possible for minors to have access to family planning without parental consent, when, in the judgment of the physician and the unmarried mother, family planning is advisable and legally possible.

In some states Planned Parenthood centers and maternal and child health services, as well as some hospitals, have assumed leadership in the organization and delivery of contraceptive information and supplies. Social agencies may wish to develop collaborative arrangements with these facilities for mutually effective service.

Social Work and Medical Services

4.10 Responsibility of the social worker during prenatal period

The social worker should help the prospective mother who comes to a social agency first to make use of medical services, and where necessary should assist the mother to obtain medical care.

> The social worker should be alert to the importance of early and continuing prenatal care and hospitalization, and should assist the unmarried mother to get the needed care from a public, private or voluntary facility.

> Where a private physician is used or where there is no social service department in the hospital or clinic, the social worker may help the unmarried mother to explain to the doctor what he needs to know about the prospective mother's social situation to understand any special needs, attitudes, problems and feelings. (4.21)

> It is important to have good communication between the doctor, the unmarried mother and the social worker to ensure that recommendations for prenatal care such as diet, exercise and specialized treatment are implemented. Nursing staff and public health nurses may be responsible for interpreting such recommendations and for helping the mother implement them.

4.11 Cooperation with the hospital at the time of confinement

To help the unmarried mother obtain adequate medical care during confinement, the social worker providing services must know the hospital policies in the community and cooperate with hospitals. (4.6)

> If there is a social service department, the agency should work with it. If not, the social worker should interpret individual situations to hospital personnel whenever the need arises.

> The social worker should help the prospective mother to provide information so that the hospital can determine whether she is eligible for its services.

> The social worker should help the unmarried mother complete a plan by the time she and her baby leave the hospital. The hospital should not be expected to provide hospitalization for either mother or baby beyond the period when it is medically necessary.

> It is the social agency's responsibility to see that the hospital is aware of the policies and procedures of the social agency. The agency also has a responsibility to maintain effective communication with the hospital, so that it may appropriately utilize the agency's resources.

> Provision of appropriate resources by the social agency for the care of newborn children is of benefit to the child and enhances cooperation between hospitals and social agencies. A hospital nursery is not a suitable facility for the care of a well baby beyond the newborn period.

4.12 Cooperative social work

When social work responsibility is shared by the agency and the hospital or clinic, careful planning and communication should take place to avoid duplication or conflict. It is also important to avoid a dilution of the social work relationship through intervention of an unnecessarily large number of persons in the major area of planning for the mother and baby. (4.21, 5.12)

Cooperative social work responsibility can best be carried out when

- the agency worker and the prospective mother are responsible for informing the hospital when the unmarried mother is or will be a patient
- the unmarried mother and the agency worker are ready to share appropriate social information, including the prospective mother's social needs as they relate to her medical care and to social planning for the mother and the child
- the social worker in the hospital or clinic interprets the individual situation to medical and other hospital staff
- care after confinement is also part of joint planning among the unmarried mother, the agency and the hospital social worker. The responsibility of the agency social worker will depend on whether the unmarried mother returns to private medical care and whether she was known to hospital social service.

4.13 Payment for hospital care

The social agency has a responsibility to help the unmarried mother find the hospital care she needs and to see that adequate prenatal care is available to her even if she is unable to meet the costs. (5.13, 8.7)

Several public programs provide care free or at cost when it is needed for the unmarried mother vulnerable to health problems.

Public or privately funded health insurance may also supplement the resources of the unmarried mother, the unmarried father and their families.

Responsibility of the Hospital

To assure adequate care for the unmarried mother, hospitals need to have definite policies about their responsibilities, over and above the provision of medical services required for all pregnant women.

4.14 Responsibility of the administration

The hospital administration should define policies regarding the unmarried parents and have specified procedures for reaching them and informing them about the services that are available.

A policy statement, accepted by heads of the departments concerned, should be prepared for medical and paramedical staffs (such as nurses and dieticians), covering

- services for unmarried mothers who may want foster family care or adoption and those who plan to keep the baby
- the relationship of the hospital to social agencies serving unmarried mothers with particular respect to referrals to or from social agencies where the hospital has a social service department and where there is none.

4.15 Referral to social agency

Hospital and clinic staffs should be alerted to recognize that a patient having a baby out of wedlock usually needs help in planning, preferably before confinement, and she should have opportunities to use available social work services for her own protection and that of the child.

This is a protection to the hospital as well as to the unmarried mother and child, since it avoids the hospital disruption that frequently results when a patient reveals lack of planning for her baby and herself at the time of discharge.

When she comes to the clinic first to confirm her pregnancy she should be offered the help of a social worker or agency in planning for her total situation.

If the patient has had no contact with a social agency and wants help, referral to the appropriate agency should be made through the social service department of the hospital. (4.21)

Unmarried mothers who are not known to a hospital or social agency until the confinement should receive special attention to determine if social work services and referral would be helpful. (2.1, 4.21)

When there is no social worker, the hospital should designate one staff person to be responsible for knowing about resources and making referrals.

Where state law requires routine reporting of unmarried mothers to the state department of welfare or reporting of babies discharged to someone other than the natural mother, the mother should be so informed. (2.4, 8.14)

Health divisions of community councils, hospital associations, public health departments and medical groups are appropriate channels for reaching hospitals without social service departments and interpreting the feasibility of referral to social agencies.

4.16 Staff education

The hospital should take steps to enhance understanding among medical and other hospital staff involved in the medical care of the unmarried mother of the special problems, attitudes, feelings and needs of the unmarried mother, and to assure staff support of overall planning for her and for the child.

4.17 Respect for the mother's wishes

Medical and nursing staff and other hospital personnel should respect the plans and wishes of the unmarried mother and recognize that she and her baby have the same rights as any other mother and her baby.

Her wish to see or not to see the child, to nurse or not to nurse the child, or for the unmarried father and other family members to see or not see the child should be respected.

4.18 Confidentiality

It is essential to assure the unmarried mother entering a hospital that her privacy with respect to her marital status will be respected and to make every effort to avoid making her or her child conspicuous.

This may involve special planning and modification of hospital procedures. It may involve careful selection of a hospital roommate or a private room, but should not include isolation of the mother or singling out of the child.

Hospital staff should avoid questions about her marital status, the absence of a visiting husband or other family members.

The need for maintaining privacy should be stressed in orientation of nursing and medical staff and of business staff and other employees who may come in contact with the patient or with records pertaining to patient care. For example, staff would not provide newspaper items about the child's birth or the mother's hospitalization, or arrange for the mother's name to be given to business companies against her wishes.

4.19 Independent adoptions

The hospital staff should avoid involvement in plans for independent adoption.

In some states, placement of a child through a third person such as hospital staff or doctors is prohibited by law. The hospital is obligated to observe this law. Where direct placement for adoption by the parent is permitted, the hospital has an ethical obligation to urge medical and other staff not to influence the unmarried mother to make an independent adoptive placement.

In some hospitals participation in unauthorized adoptions is cause for dismissal of hospital personnel, and for appropriate disciplinary action against medical staff.

Hospital staff who are in contact with patients should be well informed about desirable adoption practices. They should be familiar with laws and procedures and able to interpret them. Where independent placement by the mother is legally sanctioned, such safeguards as the law provides should prevail, as, for example, properly executed dismissal forms giving the mother's consent for release of custody of the child to the designated person.

4.20 Medical report

The hospital or physician should furnish the social agency providing service for the mother and child a prompt report of the birth history of the child and the medical history and findings on both mother and the child.

Detailed medical records should be available to medical staff responsible for followup services.

The report can be invaluable to the agency in fostering sound health practices for the new mother and in planning suitably and promptly for the baby's care, either with the mother or in a substitute family.

Where a hospital works with more than one agency, it is expedient for all to arrive at an agreement about information considered essential and to consolidate it in a single form acceptable to all the agencies.

Arrangements for obtaining written permission from the mother to furnish a medical report should be worked out between the hospital and the agency. The type of material available for a report and the need for a written request from the agency will depend on whether the hospital has a social service department and whether there has been a cooperative working relationship while the mother was under care.

4.21 Responsibility of social worker in hospital

The hospital social worker and the social agency worker should help the unmarried mother to use the hospital services in the most constructive and effective way.

The hospital social worker has intimate knowledge of the hospital, its philosophy, its policies and methods of operation, and of the various professional and other personnel within the institution who carry out the institution's responsibility for total patient care.

Interpretation of the use of social services in total medical care and planning is more effective in hospitals employing social workers.

The hospital social worker may be the first person who has contact with the unmarried mother. The hospital social worker then has responsibility for

- support, understanding and assurance that services are available
- careful evaluation of the unmarried mother's needs
- selection of and referral to the appropriate service, based on her needs as revealed in the evaluation, i.e., living arrangements, adoption service, counseling, shelter care, financial assistance, education
- preparation for the most effective use of the service at the point of referral.

The hospital social worker can interpret the special needs of the unmarried mother to the medical staff.

The hospital social worker can arrange appropriate referrals within the hospital and in the community and keep these resources advised of medical recommendations and emergencies that may arise during pregnancy and

confinement and postpartum care, as well as any changes of plan. Where indicated, she may interpret the hospital and its services to other social agencies and community organizations.

The services of the hospital social worker should be available for private patients as well as for those who come through clinics or referral from other social agencies.

When a specialized social service for unmarried parents is not available or a referral to an agency is not accepted, it is advisable for the hospital social worker to offer social work to the unmarried mother and her family. When help is needed in planning temporary placement or adoption of the child, the community agencies should be prepared to provide the service.

Other Health Services

4.22 Responsibility of community health agencies

Community health agencies such as maternal and infant care centers, family planning centers, visiting nurses, well-baby clinics or child health conferences, school health services or public health departments should also be responsible for identifying unmarried parents and children who may need help, for referrals to social agencies where indicated, and for followup services for the health of mothers and infants.

Public health agencies have a responsibility to reach out to the mother who may not come to a social agency, particularly those who are drug-dependent, those with venereal disease, the alcoholic and the mentally inadequate mother.

The high rate of prematurity among out-of-wedlock births and the rate of maternal mortality among unmarried women constitute an ongoing medical and public health problem.

5

USE OF OTHER SERVICES AND RESOURCES

The social agency needs to consider the individual needs of unmarried parents and the resources that might be used by or in behalf of the unmarried parent and child. The social worker must be involved at times in providing cooperative services, and should be responsible for coordinating and integrating the services that the parents and child receive.

Agency Consultants and Specialists

Although the social agency may carry primary responsibility for the provision of service, professional consultants should be available to the agency for direct help to unmarried parents and for consultation to staff. These consultants include physicians, nurses, pyschiatrists, psychologists, teachers, vocational guidance and employment counselors, nutritionists, lawyers and religious counselors.

5.1 Role of consultants

Specialized knowledge, experience and skills of other professions should be used in providing services for individual unmarried parents and their children and for the implementation of a total service. (7.31, 7.32)

Other professions may be called upon for

- a diagnostic clarification
- planning for special needs and problems of individuals and groups (physical, emotional, educational, religious and recreational)
- direct work with the parents or family, individually and in groups, as part of the social work plan
- consultation with social work staff
- staff development.

Consultants should provide information and professional assistance in their specific fields of competence. Consultation should help the social worker to arrive at and carry out decisions and to use social work knowledge and skill more effectively in serving unmarried parents and their children.

The specialist, in his role as teacher or consultant, also helps the social worker to understand particular aspects of an individual unmarried parent's situation.

The social worker is responsible for determining when services of the consultant are needed.

Case management and decisions within the framework of agency policy and administrative organization are the responsibility of the social work staff.

5.2 Use of specialist by parent

Based on the social work plan, arrangements may be made for the unmarried parent to make direct use of a specialist as part of the service.

The social worker should discuss with the unmarried parent the possibilities of using another professional service and should help with the decision about whether to use it.

5.3 Cooperation of social worker and specialist

When the service for the unmarried parent requires the use of other specialists, it is necessary to establish procedures that will make it possible for the parent to experience the relationships with the social worker and the specialist as complementary and consistent.

Time should be scheduled for the social worker and the specialist to discuss and agree upon the service, to exchange and evaluate the experience each has with the parent, each has with the mother or father, and to arrive at a common understanding of the plan.

The specialist has to implement the overall plan in his part of the service so that the parent using the specialist for a specific purpose, such as psychiatric treatment, understands that it is given as part of the agency service. If the social worker has a concurrent relationship with the parent, this relationship should be used to facilitate rather than to control the parent's use of the specialist.

5.4 The role of the physician

The services of obstetricians and gynecologists are used to provide medical care; to interpret the health and medical history and findings of the pregnancy, childbirth and postpartum care; to consider, treat and interpret the special health needs; to give advice about the implementation of the medical recommendations; and to interpret health needs of the mother or child to other community resources. (4.1 - 4.22)

Under the physician's supervision, the social worker may explain findings and recommendations to the mother or to others in the community who are associated with the services to the unmarried parent.

A geneticist may be helpful where questions about the heredity of the child are of concern.

5.5   The role of the nurse

Nursing services should be an integral part of a total service for the unmarried mother, particularly for those who keep their children, and should include home visits, maternity and infant care classes and pediatric counseling.

Nurses may also provide instruction in the physical aspects of pregnancy, childbirth and family planning.

5.6   The role of the psychiatrist

Psychiatric consultation should be used when needed by social work staff to clarify the psychic factors bearing on the unmarried parent's conflict, anxiety and social behavior. In addition, the psychiatrist should be used selectively to diagnose emotional disturbances or other personality disorders of an unmarried parent and when necessary to provide psychiatric treatment of an unmarried parent, or consultation.

The psychiatrist can help staff to use mental health concepts and to identify significant patterns of behavior, as a part of inservice training.

5.7   Role of the attorney

The lawyer should provide legal services and counseling, when necessary, for the unmarried parent regarding the legal consequences of keeping or giving up the child and the legal rights and responsibilities of the unmarried father and mother. (3.10)

An attorney may also advise the agency on needed legislation.

If the unmarried mother relinquishes her child for adoption, the lawyer must be sure that all legal requirements are met.

When an attorney is engaged by the agency, the attorney needs to be fully aware of the needs of the agency and available for services without being involved in a practice that is contrary to the interest of the agency.

5.8   Role of the psychologist

In appropriate situations the clinical psychologist is used to administer and interpret psychometric and projective tests; to give consultation on vocational planning; to assist on planning for remedial education; and, if qualified, to provide psychotherapy for the parents. He may also participate in inservice training programs.

5.9 Role of the religious counselor

The minister, priest or rabbi may serve as an agency consultant in matters dealing with religion. He can give support to the agency staff worker in situations in which the parents have a need for spiritual guidance and with parents who have religious problems, as well as in those individual situations in which religion may be a beneficial force to the unmarried parent.

5.10 Role of the educational specialist

Educators with special training may be consultants in planning for the education of the unmarried parents with learning problems and of school dropouts. These educators may provide remedial education, tutoring and other special services.

5.11 Role of the nutritionist

The nutritionist may be called on to work directly with the parent regarding problems in nutrition and the preparation of food or may provide consultation to the social worker or other staff member who is working with the unmarried mother.

Consultation from a home economist should be available to the nutritionist as needed.

Other Community Services

A social work service for unmarried parents is concerned not only with providing help for specific problems, but with seeing that the parents and their children have what they need for optimum development. For this reason it entails collaboration with many types of organizations: income maintenance, health, educational, religious, legal, housing, employment, recreation, and other child welfare and family services. It is necessary for social workers to be informed about community resources and to cooperate with other social agencies, organizations and institutions. The parents may need help in integrating experiences in various settings as they cope with pregnancy and birth out of wedlock.

5.12 Coordination with other community services

If the unmarried parents need or are receiving services from various community resources, the social agency should establish procedures so that the social worker providing the service for the unmarried parents participates appropriately with other facilities in the process of assessment, planning and cooperative service. (1.4)

Each professional person or organization that is associated with the unmarried parent in a significant way has something to contribute to an understanding of the unmarried parent and the psychosocial situation. The agency must develop procedures, such as periodic case conferences, to make possible the contributions of those who are involved:

- a common understanding of the psychosocial situation and the factors contributing to the need for help
- agreement on a common plan for help
- agreement on the respective responsibilities of the different services and persons involved in the overall plan
- exchange of information and sharing of experiences among cooperating members
- regular evaluation of the parent's situation, of the methods used, and of the purpose and results of the service.

5.13   Financial assistance

The social agency should assist the unmarried parents to obtain financial assistance when such help is necessary to enable them to provide the essentails to care for themselves and their children. (8.7)

It is important to distinguish between those who need financial aid and those who need both money and specialized services. For some parents, the method of help may be to supply or supplement money income only. Others may need assistance in assessing or planning better use of their own financial resources, such as budgeting, managing money, marketing or obtaining better housing. Many parents, in addition to financial assistance, may need support in caring for their children and providing a home in which the children can grow up, or help in resolving or coping with physical, social, emotional and financial problems that interfere with parental functioning and well-being.

Social service cannot be a substitute for sufficient income and a basic standard of living. For the parent, lack of income not only may mean a lack of essentials for prenatal care and normal delivery; it may seriously affect the health and well-being of the mother and child.

Financial aid should be available as a legal right to all who need it and should not be withheld or interrupted for any reasons other than those related to need. There is evidence that the use of financial assistance as a social control for unmarried parenthood does not reduce out-of-wedlock births and in fact may work a hardship on the mother and child.

Financial assistance means the provision of money in sufficient amounts to ensure regular income to meet the current expense of care of the child, housing, nutritional needs, clothing, medical care and other essential expenditures. The essential expenditures are those that enable the parents to maintain their dignity and self-respect.

5.14 Cooperation with schools and school services

The social agency should cooperate with the school staff (the principal, teachers, school nurse, guidance counselors, school social worker and visiting teacher) when an unmarried parent is having difficulties in the school.

Such difficulties include, for example, learning problems or medical problems, or the need for remedial or special education to continue an educational career.

In dealing with the unmarried parent's situation, the social situation or with special problems, the social agency staff may need to consult with personnel in the school to determine the need for special arrangements or services, to help to decide on educational goals or to arrange for special classes. Cooperation with the school makes it possible for those working with the school-age parents to exchange experiences, to understand the situation better and to involve the mother in using available services.

5.15 Vocational counseling

The social agency should seek opportunities to assist the unmarried parent who needs to develop skills for employment or improve employment skills through further training in accordance with the social work plan.

Counseling services to help determine skills and aptitudes may be a significant aspect of job security for the unmarried parent.

5.16 Day care services

A day care service, preferable family day care for the infant, should be available to the unmarried mother who keeps her child and wishes to complete her education or go to work.

Day care arrangements should be determined by the needs of the child and provided in accordance with the *CWLA Standards for Day Care Service.*

5.17 Family planning services

Family planning services should be made available, free from any coercion, to all unmarried mothers and fathers who wish to use them. (4.9)

The social agency that provides services for unmarried parents should be well informed about birth control resources and be prepared to acquaint the unmarried parents with the existing community resources.

The social agency that assists the unmarried parent with control of fertility and of childbirth should provide

- informational activities
- referral to appropriate resources

- practical assistance to effect the referral
- counseling
- followup on the referral.

Acceptance of family planning services should not be a prerequisite or requirement for public assistance or social services.

5.18 Homemaker services

Homemaker service should be available for children who may be deprived of proper care because of family circumstances and whose individual needs can best be met in their own homes.

During periods of crisis or brief parental absence from the home, such as childbirth, when the mother's other children need care and protection, homemaker service may obviate the need for temporary child placement.

5.19 Cooperation with group programs

Unmarried parents should be given opportunities to participate in group programs.

For personal development and social skills, it is often necessary for the unmarried parent to have some identification with groups and group experiences. The settlement house, recreational programs, educational programs, special activities groups and interest groups can facilitate identification with a group and functioning in groups. Participation in sectarian·groups and affiliation with religious groups and congregations can also serve this purpose.

Under supervision of professional social workers, volunteer groups can serve as a bridge between parent and the community, particularly for the parent who has to achieve or strengthen an adult role model through identification and through informal education.

6

LIVING ARRANGEMENTS FOR THE UNMARRIED MOTHER*

Assistance in making living arrangements during pregnancy and after delivery is an essential part of social services to the unmarried mother. It should be possible for her to have a choice of remaining with her own family, living in an apartment, in a foster family home, wage or companion home, maternity residence, or in a group or group care facility.

Group facilities may serve as a resource for housing or may be part of a social agency responsible for providing a total service to unmarried parents, as defined in these standards, including residential care.

6.1 Selection of living arrangements

A living arrangement should be selected in accordance with a social work plan based on careful assessment with the unmarried mother of her needs and on the formulation of short- and long-term goals.

The advantages in each arrangement should be used selectively to further her well-being and the goals of the social work plan.

The availability or agency use of only one kind of resource is not an acceptable basis for making living arrangements.

6.2 Remaining with own family

The social worker should assist the expectant mother to remain with her own family whenever such a plan contributes to her well-being and, later, to the well-being of her child.

Such an arrangement is especially suitable when the family is in accord with the unmarried mother's plan, plans with her, and accepts and supports her during her pregnancy and after the birth of her child.

---

*This section is not intended as a comprehensive standard for residential care, but pertains primarily to program. Services as noted in other sections are equally applicable to unmarried mothers who are in residential care.

6.3 Maintaining own apartment

Some expectant or unmarried mothers who have lived away from their families and have been self-supporting should be helped during pregnancy and after the child's birth to continue to live independently and maintain their own apartments.

In some instances young women can remain employed during part of their pregnancy and, with adequate care for the child, can seek reemployment following the child's birth.

The availability of housing close to medical facilities and suitable care for the child is important for the mother who keeps her child.

6.4 Financial assistance

Financial assistance should be available to unmarried expectant and actual mothers who maintain independent living arrangements and who can carry out this plan without detriment to themselves or the children. (5.13)

Foster Family Care
6.5 Use of foster family home

Specially selected and supervised foster family homes should be used during pregnancy and following confinement for unmarried mothers who need and can benefit from the experience of family living or who want the seclusion of a private home.

Foster family care can be adapted to the needs of different girls and women including

- the dependent young girl who requires carefully planned family living, extensive mothering and supervision
- the immature adolsecent who needs placement at a very early period in her pregnancy
- the woman such as the young adult who has been economically independent but needs help to carry major responsibility for her own planning during pregnancy.
- the emotionally disturbed girl whose conflicts are expressed in behavior that would be disruptive at home with her family
- the young unmarried mother and her child who require a family situation while the mother prepares for independent status.

6.6 Study and supervision of foster family homes

The agency should select foster family homes on the basis of careful study and evaluation and should provide supervision while an unmarried mother is placed in the home.

Foster family homes used by social agencies should meet the licensing requirements of the community. Each home should offer the unmarried mother living conditions with acceptable standards of health and decency, including a room of her own for rest and privacy.

Although flexibility is possible in family living, it is necessary to formulate certain policies that meet the needs of the family and the expectant or unmarried mother. Regulations about housekeeping chores for herself and the family and about visitors in the home are often necessary. The foster mother should understand and agree to her responsibilities, which may include supervision, clinic visits and recreational activities.

Experienced social work staff should be used to study and supervise foster family homes.

6.7 Personal qualifications of foster parents

The agency should select foster parents who have personal qualities enabling them to accept the unmarried pregnant girl or mother without overidentifying with her or the baby, and to work cooperatively with the agency in accordance with a social work plan.

The unmarried mother needs an atmosphere of acceptance and respect that will be supportive. This acceptance must be conveyed both to her and to the general community.

The foster parents must have a firmly established and mature relationship and be able to handle emotional upsets and crises with consistency and without undue disturbance. When children are in the home, the foster parents should have the ability to discuss and answer questions raised by the presence of the unmarried mother in the home.

The foster family must be able to refrain from imposing their own ideas on the unmarried mother, and from undue persuasion in the plan she works out with the social worker. The family must be able to accept the time limitations of the placement and to gear their role to the social work plan.

6.8 Payment for care

Foster family care for the unmarried mother should be provided in homes that receive payment from the agency in accordance with an established cost.

Responsibility for payments and incidental costs must rest with the agency.

The unmarried mother who can contribute part or all of the cost of care should make payments to the agency and not directly to the foster family. In this way the payments do not become an issue between the unmarried mother and the foster family.

6.9   Companion and wage homes

Companion homes (in which board and lodging are provided in return for specified responsibilities) and wage homes (in which a small salary is paid in addition to board and lodging) should be carefully studied, selected and supervised and should be used with discrimination on the basis of a social work plan.

Agencies should have standards for these homes that meet the individual needs of the situation and assure a good quality of care.

On occasion such homes may be considered for the expectant mother who wishes to establish some degree of independence and assume either total or part financial responsibility for herself and for whom other suitable employment is not available because of her pregnancy.

The agency should establish minimum wage rates for the services provided, as guidelines for the foster parent and the unmarried mother in wage homes.

Companion and wage homes should not be used as a way for an agency to save money nor to obtain homes by providing inexpensive household help.

6.10   Parent-child homes

Foster family homes in which the mother and child live together while the mother works or attends school should be used with special care.

Foster parents who assist the unmarried mother through example and instruction in the skills and techniques of parenting are helpful to new mothers. Such homes give the mother the opportunity to learn and to experience the responsibility of caring for a child, with some assistance from the foster family.

The responsibility the mother assumes for herself and her baby, such as purchase and preparation of food for herself and the child and care of her child, can provide a realistic basis for her to decide whether she wishes to continue to care for her child or terminate parental rights.

Group Living Facilities

The nature and role of group living facilities have become more varied with the growth in knowledge and understanding of the problems and needs of the unmarried mother, the development of skills in assessment and amelioration of social and emotional problems, and greater cooperation with other community services. The residence of early days was designed to afford environmental and spiritual security and an assurance of confidentiality, and to provide physical care, medical attention and moral training of the unmarried pregnant mother. The basic purpose of group living facilities is still to provide a living arrangement that meets the individual needs of the unmarried mother, but without shutting her off from the community.

50

6.11 Use of group living facility

Group residences should be used for the girl who prefers group living, and whose needs can best be met in a regulated environment that provides a group living experience, a diversified program, treatment and rehabilitation opportunities for problems associated with pregnancy and early motherhood.

6.12 Characteristics of group care

Residential group care should offer the unmarried mother some of the following advantages:

- the security, guidance and support she may need to prepare herself for the physical, social and emotional responsibilities of pregnancy, childbirth and motherhood, and, when appropriate, care and protection of the child.
- a program to meet her emotional, physical, educational, vocational, recreational and spiritual needs
- opportunities for personal growth through supervised group living experiences and creative activities
- treatment of emotional problems through planned use of its resources and services.

A group living facility can afford assurance of privacy and can meet the wish to conceal the pregnancy.

These settings can provide a regulated environment from which some girls can derive security, especially those for whom the availability of 24-hour-a-day staff services is important. At the same time, they allow for freedom in a controlled and protected environment.

They provide a medium for the development of sound group programs and therapeutic groups, with leadership of a person skilled in handling group processes to promote social work goals.

Group living presents opportunities in which the individual can act out and test feelings and relationships, and find acceptance. Planned grouping allows for constructive interacting group relationships with peers and adults.

The interrelationship of staff and their observations contribute to better understanding of the individual and to an integrated service plan.

An activity program offers a number of choices in such areas as education, skills development, socialization, arts and crafts, for the development of self-expression, recognition of ability and creativity. The individual is able to test herself in a variety of work experiences out of which may grow greater appreciation of self in relation to society.

The existence of the group living facility represents to the girl seeking its services society's concern for the individual as a person of worth and value. This is of immeasurable value to each person in the group.

6.13 Auspices of the group living facility

It is preferable for a group living facility to be under the auspices of, or part of, an authorized social agency providing service for unmarried parents.

A residential facility may also provide specialized services for unmarried prospective mothers in the community.

It may also serve as a central community resource offering residential care that is used or purchased by other agencies carrying primary responsibility for services for unmarried parents.

6.14 Maternity homes

The maternity home should be used for unmarried mothers who need a structured group living experience and those related professional services necessary for comprehensive care of the girl during pregnancy and in some circumstances after the infant's birth.

Many program variations arise from such factors as size of the home, geographic location, adequacy of financing, the availability of services, and the community's needs.

6.15 Group homes

Small, decentralized units in the community, such as agency-administered group homes or apartments, should be available for pregnant women and unmarried mothers who cannot live with their own families or return to their homes but do not wish to be alone or with a foster family; this arrangement can serve as a transition between life in their own families and entry into an independent life situation.

This form of group care has particular benefits to the youthful girl or mother who can use special help as she moves into independence.

Some adolescents in their mid-teens who have to leave their own homes for the first time can adjust better to the less intimate adult-child relationships of a group home than to foster family care.

6.16 Cooperative living arrangements

Social agencies, when requested, should be ready to provide specialized social services to the groups of self-supporting unmarried mothers who develop living arrangements that include several unrelated unmarried parents and their children.

Services such as assistance with the planning of a good child care program that the residents implement can help the parents plan for the care and protection of their children.

6.17 Day care of infants*

When a day care program is provided in a group living facility to enable the mother to continue her education or participate in job training, it should meet the requirements of any day care program for infants.

Family day care is a desirable arrangement for the care of infants.

6.18 Licensing of group living facilities

All group living facilities administered by social agencies should be licensed or authorized to operate by an appropriate state agency and should meet state licensing requirements for health and safety.

Jurisdiction and requirements for licensing of a residential facility are dependent on the scope of the activities of the home. In general, licensing will involve different state departments that regulate minimum standards of care. When the facility is subject to the jurisdiction of several state departments, each department should assume responsibility for licensing the facilities used for that particular component of service.

The following considerations are determinants of licensing jurisdiction:

- If the group living facility admits girls in the age group for which state law requires licensing as a child care facility, or cares for their babies, it should be licensed by the state department as a child welfare service.

- No maternity home should be licensed to provide residential care for infants after the mother has been discharged. Foster family homes should be used for the care of infants in these instances.

- When day care is provided, the service should meet the licensing requirements for a day care facility.

- If a group living facility provides foster family care or adoption service, it should also be required to be licensed as a child placement agency.

- If a group living facility provides medical treatment, nursing care and hospital services, it should be subject to the licensing jurisdiction of the state department of health as well as to review by proper accrediting bodies in the practice of medicine and hospital administration.

Responsibility of the Social Agency That Administers Maternity Homes or Group Living Facilities

6.19 Residential care

Residential care provided in a maternity home or other group living facility, including shelter, physical care, group living experience, and individual and group work relationships, should be used selectively and coordinated with the social work

---

*See *CWLA Standards for Day Care Service, Revised.*

plan and medical program according to the needs and problems of the individual unmarried mother and child.

6.20   Social work in a group living facility

Responsibility for continuing social work as an integral part of the service for the unmarried mother for as long as she needs it should be designated, whether it is carried by the social worker of the home itself, a social worker in the social agency of which it is a part, or a social worker of an agency that arranged for the unmarried mother to use a group living facility. The social worker in the residence has a specific responsibility for helping the individual make the best use of residential care.

Individualized services should be complemented by group activities and group discussions.

The social worker should assist the unmarried mother with adjustment to and use of the living experience in the maternity home or group residence, coordinate services within and outside of the home for each girl in accordance with the social work plan, and interpret the use of the home to other staff of the agency and to other social agencies and community resources.

Some of the problems that all unmarried mothers share can be discussed in informal group meetings, at which attendance is voluntary. Joint discussion of mutual problems can give the helping process an added dimension. The social worker who leads discussion groups should have a thorough knowledge of the group work method and be familiar with modern social work concepts concerning problems and care of unmarried mothers.

6.21   Educational activities

Educational activities should be planned in accordance with the needs of the individual unmarried mother and the social work plan for her.

Formal academic instruction should be available for the unmarried school-age pupil during pregnancy and after the birth of the child, unless contraindicated for medical reasons. Arrangements should be made through the local board of education for accredited instruction, to ensure that credit will be given for work completed. Safeguards may be necessary to assure that information about the girl will be kept confidential if her credits are to be transferred.

Vocational skills should be primarily concerned with the development of appropriate skills to obtain employment, and may also include skills such as homemaking.

Family life education should be available to all residents, and instruction in care of infants should be given to unmarried mothers who keep their babies. (8.8)

6.22 Medical services

Medical and hospital care should be obtained through arrangement with community medical and hospital facilities, or it may be part of a maternity home program provided that in quality it corresponds to acceptable medical care available through other community resources. (4.1 − 4.22)

Arrangements for medical services should assure continuity of health and medical care and a social work service.

Policies and Procedures

The policies and procedures of a group living facility must carry out the purpose of its services for unmarried parents. They should be carefully drawn up and subject to constant reevaluation in the light of changing needs.

6.23 Admission policy

The basis of eligibility for residential care should be the ability to use the available services.

Homes under religious auspices or those set up to serve a particular group or special social problem should define their admission policies clearly. In general, policies should state that no application should be rejected because of race, color, legal residence, prior marital status, prior pregnancy, economic status or ability to pay.

If the agency cannot provide the necessary and appropriate living arrangements, policy should provide for referral to other community resources that can better meet the needs of the young woman.

It is difficult for an unmarried mother to enter a residence until she recognizes her need for help. Therefore, policies should not require her to be admitted at any specified stage of pregnancy. Nor should eligibility depend upon the plan she has for her child or her willingness to remain in the group residence for any specified period of time beyond that required for the achievement of the social work plan or appropriate medical care.

The social worker in a group living facility, in consultation with the administrator or supervisory staff or both, should make the decision whether to accept an applicant for residential care on the basis of the needs and problems of the applicant, the makeup of the group currently in residence, and the nature of the service.

6.24 Payments

The unmarried mother who uses residential care should be expected to pay the agency in accordance with her ability for expenses of living arrangements and medical care, other expenses for the child, and additional services rendered.

Financial arrangements should assure stability of placement for the unmarried mother and infant. The costs may include higher rates after the child is born.

Ability to pay should be determined on the basis of current circumstances.

Other members of the family and the unmarried father may assist the unmarried mother to meet the costs of care.

6.25 House rules

The group facility should define for and with the residents the requirements in a group living situation that are essential to permit orderly maintenance of the home.

These should allow for maximum personal freedom within necessary limits and for flexibility in making reasonable adjustments.

6.26 Work assignments

Work assignments should be considered and planned as an integral part of the total social work program and should be geared to the physical health, educational and vocational needs, as well as the emotional well-being, of the pregnant or actual mother.

The work program should not be used as a substitute for financing adequate staff.

Staff of the Group Living Facility

The kind and number of staff depend upon the number of mothers and babies cared for, the kind of services provided directly by the group home, the services obtained through other community resources, the administrative structure and the physical plant.

The quality of the services for the unmarried mother and the child is dependent largely on the personal qualifications, knowledge and skill of staff.

6.27 Size of staff

There should be a sufficient number of qualified staff to perform effectively the tasks required in providing the total service for the unmarried mother accepted for care and for her child.

The number of staff and the positions required should be determined by the size and purpose of the residence.

Not all residences will need all categories of staff. The responsibilities should be listed for the various positions and be assigned to members of the staff who are qualified to carry them.

Staff members who are in close and intimate contact with the unmarried mother should have warmth and understanding of her, knowledge of prenatal care and childbirth, and an ability to identify with the philosophy and goals of the agency in which they are employed.

Professional staff should meet the standards for competence in their particular field. Both professional and nonprofessional staff should have the personal qualifications necessary for the complex task of working with expectant and actual unmarried mothers.

Buildings and Grounds

The design of the physical facilities of a group living facility should be functional in relation to its program and promote the objectives of the services it offers. Physical facilities and living arrangements can affect the quality of the services that are provided and the ability of the resident to use them to the fullest benefit. The environment should enhance her feeling of self-respect and her capacity to relate positively to other people in her world.

6.28 Physical plant

Living facilities should meet the varying needs of the young women served and be in accordance with the nature of the program.

Such facilities include maternity homes, group homes or apartments. Arrangements may take different forms depending upon available space and nature of the program.

In building and remodeling physical facilities, the agency should consult appropriate authorities and experts for optimum standards to be incorporated into building plans. These include not only architects, but directors of group living facilities and state licensing consultants.

6.29 Location

The group living facility should be easily accessible to services and facilities needed by the residents.

Good transportation is essential.

7

ORGANIZATION AND ADMINISTRATION OF SOCIAL AGENCIES PROVIDING SOCIAL SERVICES FOR UNMARRIED PARENTS

Unmarried parents and their children require multiple resources and services of various agencies and professions. The social agency can coordinate the various services that they may need by combining some of these within one organization, and by maintaining a close working relationship with agencies, facilities and individuals providing other services.

The organization and administration of the agency that offers services for unmarried parents and their children determine to a large extent the quality of the services offered. The extent to which effective services can be offered depends upon the caliber, conviction and understanding of the board of directors, the adequacy of agency financing, the availability and integration of necessary resources in the community, and the knowledge, skill and professional qualifications of the staff.

7.1 Auspices of services

The agency may be under public auspices or under private auspices (religious or nonsectarian).

7.2 Authorization

The voluntary agency should be incorporated under state and local requirements and should operate under a charter and bylaws that authorize service for unmarried parents. The public agency should be properly authorized by statute to offer its service and should function in conformity with statutory requirements. (8.15, 8.22, 8.23)

7.3 Purposes and objectives

The agency should have a written statement setting forth its purpose and objectives and the specific services that it offers. The extent of the agency's service for unmarried parents should be planned in concert with other agencies and organizations in relation to the community's available and necessary services for child welfare needs.

7.4 Maintenance of standards

Each agency should continually evaluate its functions, policies and practices on the basis of established standards and the existing need in both the state and local community.

> The same standards of practice or service should apply to all agencies regardless of auspices.

7.5 Relation to the community

The agency should engage in activities to achieve sound interagency relationships and participate in both community planning and social action to bring about a coordinated public and voluntary program for unmarried parents. (8.1 – 8.2)

> A service for unmarried parents is a specialized service that can carry out its purposes only as an integral part of a total community program of services for families and children.

> The agency should determine whether existing legislation and court procedures offer adequate protection for unmarried parents and their children; make known and interpret any need for revisions; support those measures that will assure the services and protections required; and oppose those that are contrary to the best interest of the child or the unmarried parent.

Participation in Social Planning
7.6 Responsibility for social action

The agency responsible for the provision of social work services for unmarried parents must also engage in social action to help change unfavorable community conditions that it encounters, to develop community resources that are needed and to work with community planning groups and citizen groups. (8.3)

> Out of its daily experience, the social agency can contribute facts about community needs and identify the lack of resources that affect the children born out of wedlock and their parents.

> There should be channels of communication from staff members to the executive director and the board to keep them informed of community conditions that need to be changed and about which the agency should take some responsibility for stimulating appropriate community action.

When necessary, the agency should participate in the development of social policy, services and resources.

The agency may enlist unmarried parent groups that identify social problems to participate in finding a solution.

7.7 Planning and coordination

The agency has a responsibility for joining with other social agencies in the community for the purpose of coordinating, planning and expanding services for the unmarried parents and children requiring them. (8.5)

Agency board and staff have a responsibility for constant assessment and evaluation of their services so that their program may be adapted to the changing needs of the community.

The agency should participate in defining procedures for cooperative services and developing more effective ways of integrating community services.

The agency should offer leadership in the development of community resources that provide for the special needs of unmarried parents and their children. Such programs should be directed toward the improvement of economic and social conditions that adversely affect children and their parents and the security of family life, and toward the provision of services in the community that strengthen the unmarried parents and offer help to them with specific problems of family living.

7.8 Legislation

The agency has the responsibility through joint board and staff leadership to promote legislation enhancing the welfare of unmarried parents and of their children.

The Board of Directors
7.9 Responsibilities of the board

A service for unmarried parents should be conducted under the auspices of a governing body that is responsible for developing program and financial support, as well as formulating policies for services offered by the agency.

In a voluntary agency the ultimate responsibility for service lies with the board. The board should appoint the executive and delegate administrative responsibility to him. It should be responsible for establishing the policies within which the staff works, but should not participate in decisions about individuals served by the agency.

The responsibilities of the board, executive and staff should be distinct but interdependent, and should be clearly defined and understood.

The organization of the agency should provide channels that enable both the executive and staff to make contributions toward both formulation of policies and development of programs.

The functions and responsibilities of the board of a public agency depend on whether there is a commission or cabinet form of government and on the way in which responsibility for administration is placed. The board of a public agency may be administrative in the full meaning of the term as the commission or board of commissioners in some states or the board in local agencies; it may be policy making as in many state agencies where the actual administration is the responsibility of the executive appointed by the governor; or it may be advisory only, as in other states where the executive carries administrative responsibility. Regardless of its function, it should be mandatory that a nonpartisan board be appointed and be able to speak for public child welfare services.

7.10 Board composition

The board should represent the community and groups served by the agency. Membership on the board should provide for infusion of new points of view and for the representation from new groups in the community.

7.11 Qualifications of board membership

Board members should have personal qualifications that enable them both to give leadership and to carry out their responsibilities.

These qualifications should include an interest in the welfare of unmarried parents and their children, a capacity and willingness to learn the purpose and objectives of the agency's service, convictions about the necessity of providing and financing a service that meets acceptable standards, concern for social conditions in the community that affect the care of unmarried parents and their children, and time for participating fully and consistently in carrying out board responsibilities.

Financial Resources

The agency must have and should seek financial resources that will make it possible to carry out responsibility for the unmarried parents whom it accepts for care and to allow for expansion of service in accordance with community needs.

7.12 Source of funds

The services of the agency should be financed by the community through voluntary contributions and allocation of tax funds.

The possibility of obtaining public funds through federal, state and local public agencies should be considered.

Allocations from community funding bodies should be requested on the basis of an annual projected budget estimated to cover all expenses required to maintain good standards and to take into account income from payments and other resources.

An audited financial statement should be published annually.

7.13 Costs of service

Unit costs of the service should be computed and should be used as a basis for obtaining financial support, for purchasing service, and for payment schedules.

7.14 Purchase of service

It is sound practice for a public agency to purchase and a voluntary agency to sell services that parents of children born out of wedlock or the children themselves need when the public agency cannot provide it.

When public funds are paid to voluntary agencies they should be given in payment for service for individual children and families for whom the public agency has responsibility, and should cover the full cost of service.

Written contractual agreements mutually arrived at and clearly stating the responsibilities of the agencies involved should regulate purchase of services.

Responsibility for continuing casework and for planning for mother and child after birth should be decided prior to purchase of care.

Services should be available by purchase for unmarried parents who need them whether they enter residential care or remain in the community.

7.15 Payments for service

Unmarried parents should be expected to pay to the extent of their ability for the care provided them and for boarding care and other expenses for the child.

Fees for counseling during pregnancy may discourage unmarried parents from agency service, particularly if the unmarried parents do not ask for such service. For that reason, careful thought should be given to policies on fees and other payments, so that no unmarried parents or their children are deprived of the protection an agency can afford.

Service should not be denied to any unmarried parent because of inability or unwillingness to make payments.

7.16 Size and basis for payments

Payments should be based on the full cost of the total service for the child and the family and the unmarried parents.

The agency may establish a flat fee that may be waived or it may use a sliding scale and adjust payments on the basis of criteria prepared by the agency.

Policies and Procedures

Policies and procedures of the agency should be clearly formulated and consistent with basic principles of adequate service to unmarried parents and their children.

7.17 Responsibility for development of policies and procedures

Statements of policy regarding agency function, relationships with other agencies, coordination, cooperative services, personnel practices, and financing should be developed with collaboration of board and staff. Appropriate systematic procedures for carrying out policies should be developed by the executive and staff and understood and approved by the board.

It is important to establish channels of communication so that the board may have advice and consultation from the executive and the staff in developing policy. The staff's experience in carrying out the agency function and the staff's knowledge of community conditions and needs can contribute to the board's knowledge and to the development of sound policies.

Procedures need to be developed regarding agency practice, and business, stenographic, clerical and other operations.

7.18 Agency manual

Policies and procedures should be set forth in manuals, which should be available at all times to the board and staff.

Responsibility for keeping such manuals up to date rests with the executive, in consultation with staff and board.

Staffing

In a social agency, the social work staff carries primary responsibility for providing services to unmarried parents and children born out of wedlock. The staff may include social workers with graduate professional training and those with undergraduate education and agency training. Under professional supervision or direction, professionally trained staff, agency-trained staff, volunteers and neighborhood residents should be used for specified activities that are a part of the service.

7.19 Job definitions

Allocation of authority and responsibility within the agency should be clearly defined.

Job specifications are essential for each position, sufficiently comprehensive and detailed so that a person may have a clear understanding of the responsibilities of his own position, as well as those inherent in the positions of other staff members.

Although lines of authority should be clearly defined, there should be sufficient flexibility for effective intra-agency communication among all levels of administrative responsibility.

7.20 Size of staff

The staff should be sufficient in number to ensure a desirable quality of services at all times, in accordance with these standards.

Size of staff will vary from agency to agency and will depend upon the scope of the program, number of services provided directly and number of individuals served.

Professional specialists may be employed on a full- or part-time basis as members of the staff team when appropriate to the service provided. In addition, consultation may be purchased as needed to carry out the purpose of the service.

7.21 Qualifications of staff

It is desirable for social work staff, particularly directors of services for unmarried parents and social work supervisors, to have professional social work education. In addition, each staff member should possess personal qualities that enable effective working relationships with unmarried parents.

Personal qualifications to be considered in selection of staff include
- deep and sympathetic understanding of problems involved in pregnancy and parenthood out of wedlock
- recognition of own feelings about deviations from sex mores, illegitimacy, adoption and related problems.
- awareness of any need to impose one's personal values, particularly in planning for the future of a child
- respect for individuals and their right of self-determination, and acceptance of their differences.
- unusual sensitivity to feelings of others, ability to establish relationships quickly, and capacity to sustain a relationship that can become the basis for a helping process
- ability to work comfortably within the framework of established policy and procedure, to accept agency objectives, and to function in a teamwork relationship with other members of the staff and with staff employed in other social agencies.

64

7.22 Differential use of personnel

It is desirable for agencies to use personnel without professional experience or with different levels of education, and to define tasks that can be performed by them with competence. In addition, volunteers, neighborhood residents and agency-trained workers should be assigned tasks equal to their ability.

Professionally educated staff should be responsible for those tasks that require skills, judgments and decisions that involve social work knowledge, values and experience such as:

- psychosocial diagnosis
- case planning and service assessment
- selection of appropriate helping methods
- psychosocial treatment
- evaluation
- consultation.

Consideration should be given to the use of the social work team composed of staff with differing levels of education, volunteers, social work students and neighborhood residents under the leadership of the professional social worker.

Under the guidance, direction or supervision of a professional staff member, certain activities may be carried out by nonprofessional staff. The unmarried parents may need assistance with job training, the search for employment or housing, budgeting, or training in child care for those who keep their children. The agency should be prepared to use special skills that nonprofessional staff may have to enrich services for unmarried parents.

7.23 Volunteers

The agency should utilize volunteers to provide supplemental services that enrich and extend services for unmarried parents.

Volunteers should be assigned well-defined tasks that fit their abilities and that are agreeable to both the volunteer and the agency.

The orientation and training of volunteers should be planned for the maximum participation and involvement of staff and volunteers.

7.24 Work loads

The size of the work load assigned to an individual social worker or team should be determined on the basis of time required to complete satisfactorily the units of service for which the social worker is responsible.

It is necessary to take into account the time required for direct work with the unmarried parents in the office and at home and in collateral visits, emergencies, supervision, consultation and recording, as well as work with community groups, attendance at staff conferences, professional meetings and inservice training.

Staff Development

It is the responsibility of the agency to make adequate provisions for continued staff development in order to promote and improve the quality of service.

7.25 Educational program

The agency program should include staff seminars; inservice training; educational leave; attendance at professional conferences, institutes and workshops; and an adequate professional library within the agency.

7.26 Supervision

Regular supervisory help should be available to every staff member, in accordance with need and level of professional development.

It should include individual supervision, group supervision, and use of consultation by experienced caseworkers who can take responsibility for seeking help as needed.

7.27 Executive director

In addition to having the qualifications needed by all members of the social work staff, the executive director of the agency should be especially equipped by training, experience and personal qualities to establish and maintain a sound administrative structure, to carry out policies, to provide leadership for staff and board, and to give community leadership in developing resources for services to unmarried parents and their children.

7.28 Supervisory staff

The number of supervisors should be sufficient to ensure that the services of the agency meet standards of acceptable practice. The supervisory staff should have professional education, experience in child welfare services, and personal qualities that inspire the confidence of the staff and the various community agencies with which the staff works.

Supervisory staff is a key to providing competent services, particularly in agencies that employ some staff members who do not have professional social work education.

There should be one supervisor for no more than five or six social workers who need individual supervision. Peer group supervision and the use of consultation can reduce the number of supervisors needed for social work staff with professional education, experience and demonstrated competence.

Usually more supervisory time is required when the agency employs workers with little training or experience. The use of the social work team can provide the necessary supervision without greatly increasing the number of supervisory staff.

7.29 The social worker

Social workers, through their basic professional education and inservice training, should have an understanding of child development and behavior and of the physical needs and related aspects of pregnancy and childbirth; and they should have at least beginning skills in relating to individuals and groups as well as a skill in the assessment and the development of the unmarried parents' capacity for parenthood.

7.30 Office staff

Provision should be made for secretarial, stenographic, clerical and other staff as needed.

Efficient performance of social work staff is dependent upon the competence of staff throughout the agency. The office staff should be oriented to the goals of the agency and the confidential nature of the job.

7.31 Personnel policies

Conditions of work and personnel practice should be stated in writing. These include salaries, pension plans and various fringe benefits commonly accepted in present-day society, and should be comparable to the standards of the National Association of Social Workers.

Consultants
7.32 Qualifications of specialists

All specialists should meet educational and other requirements for membership in the standard-setting organization in their own professional fields. In addition, they should have personal characteristics and experience that make it possible for them to work with unmarried parents and to collaborate with other staff members.

7.33 Policies for use of specialists

There should be a well-formulated plan for use of specialists, with clarity in their role and responsibility, particularly for those who are regularly needed because of the nature of the service. (5.1)

> The services of specialists should be paid by a stated fee, by a salary, or on a retainer basis.

> It is important for the specialist to have a defined role that is consistent with agency practice and philosophy. The relationship of the specialist to the agency and the staff, the expectations and responsibilities of the specialist and the staff, and the processes through which these responsibilities are to be carried out should be specified.

> The specialists need to understand and accept the agency's purpose and methods to utilize their special competence to support agency goals. The agency needs to be clear about the particular expertise that the specialist has, and how it is to be used.

> Consultation should not be confused with or used as a substitute for supervision. Supervision should be provided on a continuous basis by agency staff.

Case Records

> To maintain continuity of service and to evaluate the service given, a case record for each individual situation should be compiled from the initial contact to the termination of service.

7.34 Compilation of records

The agency should maintain a case record of the unmarried mother and father to preserve essential information, to serve as a basis for social work planning, treatment and evaluation; and to help improve the quality of services available to unmarried parents.

> Case recording has been a matter of continuous concern and experimentation. Narrative recording, form recording or summaries are all in general use today. The basic principles of relevance, currency, economy and adequacy are essential guideposts.

> The social agency should provide clear, adequate and well-written instructions to the staff regarding what is to be recorded and how to record it. Pertinent information about the child born out of wedlock and the parents of the child, in addition to information about significant persons, should be included. In addition, evaluative summaries upon which decisions are based, medical information and any legal documents should be part of the case record.

7.35 Preservation of records

Case records should be preserved, either through microfilming or by selective retention of information and documents for a specified reasonable period, after which it is unlikely that the full record will be needed.

7.36 Confidentiality

Confidentiality should be maintained in accordance with the ethics of the social work profession and the responsibility of the agency for the best interest of the client.

Information that the agencies obtain from unmarried parents and other interested persons is generally not protected in a legal sense by the laws concerning privileged communication. Each agency, however, should determine the conditions under which staff members share information about the unmarried parents.

It is desirable to obtain the written consent of the unmarried parent to give information to other agencies or individuals. Information should be shared only where professional judgment indicates that it is in the best interests of the parent or child.

Statistics and Reporting

Agency statistics regarding the services provided for unmarried parents are essential in determination of agency policies, formulation of budgets, accountability to the public for actions and expenditures, interpretation of program and of problems to the public, identification and definition of unmet needs, and shaping of present programs or development of new programs to meet needs.

7.37 Responsibilities for statistics and reporting

The agency should keep accurate statistics that are needed in administration, community interpretation and research. (8.20)

The agency should take responsibility for participating in reporting systems and for reporting through publications or other means its experience and findings about new practices and results that may be of interest or benefit to the unmarried parents or their children.

7.38 Use of statistics

The agency should use statistical accounting to keep an accurate record of the children and unmarried parents receiving the service to unmarried parents.

It should know sources, types of problem classifications and referrals received by the agency and disposition of those situations, including those not accepted and the reasons for not accepting them.

It is important to keep statistics for specific purposes. Staff should be informed of the purpose and should see the results of the time spent in providing statistical data.

Monthly and yearly reports of needed statistical material should be prepared to show accurately the volume and type of service given by the agency and to facilitate analysis of work loads for the purpose of determining staff needs and assessing individual performance of staff.

Statistics should also be available for use in interpreting the work of the agency to the board and to the community, for assessing unmet needs, for time studies to determine work loads, for substantiating need for financial support and additional service and to provide a basis for research in specific areas of practice.

Research

7.39 Responsibility for research

It is important for agencies to participate in research projects with other agencies and national organizations to evaluate the effectiveness of practice and to extend basic knowledge about services for unmarried parents and their children; and, when feasible, to carry on independent research.

Research encompasses not only demonstration projects, but systematic gathering of data such as reasons for requests for service, kinds of service given, followup studies of special groups and their situation, work load and costs.

Services should be continually evaluated. Methods of quality control need to be developed to measure progress toward goals.

Research programs should be undertaken under supervision of qualified research personnel or in consultation with research staff of universities and other policy and planning bodies.

Appropriate safeguards to maintain confidentiality should be set up.

7.40 Funds for research

Money should be allocated for research as an item in the budget of services for unmarried parents.

Consideration should be given to outside sources of funds such as foundations and public agencies. The possibility of collaboration and sharing of budgets with universities, schools and research centers should also be considered.

Community Interpretation

Interpretation to the community is a joint responsibility of staff and board, and should be a part of the ongoing program of the agency. Interpretation can be carried out informally in the day-to-day activities of the agency and formally through efforts such as publicity campaigns and planned programs for community education.

7.41 Purpose of interpretation

Board and staff should carry on an active program of interpretation and education within the community in order

- to increase awareness of social conditions and social forces that affect children born out of wedlock and their parents
- to bring unmet needs to the attention of the community
- to bring about wider use of agency services by reaching those members of the community who have need of it
- to enlist the support of an informed citizenry
- to encourage appropriate and effective referrals for service from other community agencies and from groups who often serve as sources of referral.

7.42 Use of public relations

Services of a public relations specialist should be used within the framework of the general philosophy and the professional standards of the agency in community interpretation, fund raising and to obtain appropriations.

8

COMMUNITY PLANNING AND ORGANIZATION OF SERVICES TO UNMARRIED PARENTS

Effective services to unmarried parents depend on integration of many resources in the community. The community must provide access to basic health, education and welfare services for prevention and treatment of the social ills frequently associated with having children outside of marriage. Legislation should assure that services and resources to protect their rights and to provide for their care are available, and should define public responsibility for leadership in the promotion of adequate services for unmarried parents throughout the state under both public and voluntary auspices.

8.1 Planning and coordination of community services

For greater administrative effectiveness, services to children born outside of marriage and to their parents should be coordinated by joint planning at national, state, county and local levels among the social agencies and other organizations and facilities that provide the various components of care and services to the parents and the children.

Community planning should be directed toward increasing the availability of a complete range of services of high standards, with ample coverage for all in need of them.

Planning should pay special attention to the needs, services and gaps in service for unmarried parents, and should have as a primary goal the stimulation and coordination of services. It should also include community education, interpretation and a review of related legislation.

8.2 Public and voluntary cooperation

Responsibility for planning and provision of services to parents of children born out of wedlock is a public responsibility that should be shared with voluntary agencies and other organizations that make substantial contributions of service, staff and funds to the social problems associated with out-of-wedlock births.

Planning and coordination of services should ensure that unmarried parents will have needed services available no matter at what point they first seek service.

Public and voluntary services should be integrated or complementary to each other, so that they meet the needs within the community. Such an arrangement should provide opportunities for all who can use the services to obtain them regardless of eligibility requirements such as age, race, religious affiliation or ability to pay a fee.

8.3 Interpretation of services

Joint community efforts should be undertaken to make the available professional services known to the groups who are potential users, to neighborhood and community groups, and to professional and occupational groups likely to be involved with unmarried parents, their children and their families.

8.4 Information and referral services

Each community should have centralized and satellite sources of information about and referral to available services and resources to which the unmarried parents and their families may turn.

It is difficult for individuals in the community to be familiar with the several aspects of care that are available and necessary.

A centralized information service should include information, advice, steering, and referral service. It could be manned by a volunteer or citizen group or social work technicians. Professionally manned referral services, whether independently operated or in social agencies that make referrals to appropriate resources and services, should also employ followup and feedback mechanisms to ensure linkage for appropriate service.

8.5 Expansion of services

Agencies providing services for unmarried parents and their children should work toward the expansion of services to be available for all who can use them.

Services should be extended to a larger number of unmarried parents through planned efforts to provide maximum possibilities for the use of available services to those who have fewer opportunities to obtain help.

Services must include social supports to facilitate the ability of mothers to care adequately for their children if they so desire; therefore, services not only should cover the period of pregnancy and childbirth but, when necessary, should make provision to protect and promote the mental health of the child during the critical period after birth.

8.6 Multiple-service organizations

In areas where unmarried parents are found in large numbers, it is preferable for the community to provide a comprehensive service that meets the basic needs of health and education as well as social services, in a *one-stop* facility. (2.4)

Such a plan offers a greater possibility of care for the unmarried parents and their children who are most likely to need varying services and resources. These services should preserve the individual's right to use or reject the service, and preserve the specialized competencies of the agencies that participate.

8.7 Provision of funds

The community should allocate sufficient funds to both public and private agencies so that the unmarried parents and their children who require services may obtain from public or voluntary agencies the care and resources they need. (5.13)

No unmarried parent should be forced to forgo necessary services and resources because of insufficient personal funds.

The state department responsible for social services should be empowered to provide or to authorize programs for unmarried mothers and the children born out of wedlock prior to, during, and for a reasonable period after the birth of the child, in residential and nonresidential care.

If the public agency purchases care, the per capita cost should cover the actual cost of providing adequate services.

Social work services should be available to all unmarried mothers receiving public assistance and to those in public institutions.

Public funds provided directly to unmarried parents to pay for services may facilitate access to needed services for those who lack personal funds.

8.8 Responsibility of state board of education

School districts should be encouraged to permit unmarried school-age pregnant girls and mothers who wish to do so to remain in their regular schools.

Alternative programs for the completion of education to which they are entitled should be available to high school students who are unable to continue regular classroom instruction.

A comprehensive program of family life education, including sex education, hygiene of pregnancy and nutrition, should be available for pregnant women and school-age mothers as an integral part of a curriculum that includes a planned and sequential program of health education. (1.3, 6.21)

Legislation

The concern of society for the general welfare of its citizens is expressed in its most enduring form through social legislation. Services for unmarried parents and their children require a sound framework of social legislation. Much of this legislation is concerned with the general welfare of all citizens. However, certain enactments are specifically directed toward the welfare of unmarried parents and their children, or influence their welfare to such a marked degree that they require special attention from social agencies and citizen groups.

8.9 Rights of the child and parents

Legislation should assure that the rights of both the unmarried parents and their children are protected, and that the interests of the child are paramount when conflicts arise between the rights of the child and of the parents.

8.10 Legal status of the minor unmarried parent

Legislation should provide for provision of social services and referral for medical care without parental consent to the minor unmarried parent or pregnant girl, when, in the judgment of the physician or social agency, absence of such care would jeopardize the health or well-being of the minor.

Generally a minor will seek the interest and concern of parents and be responsive. It is recognized, however, that among some unmarried mothers fear of informing the parents of the pregnancy deters the girl from seeking service, and the hospital or social agency from providing it.

In working with a minor it is necessary to reconcile the legal rights and responsibilities of the girl's parents with the social work commitment to the care of and concern for the minor's well-being. It is recognized that it is not always in the best interest of the minor to notify the parent prior to the provision of needed services.

A minor should not be compelled to surrender her child against her will because of her status as a minor. In a case where a minor, like an adult, does not wish to give up the child but cannot recognize an inability to provide care for the child, legal action may be required to terminate her rights in her best interests as well as those of her child. (3.10)

8.11 Birth records

Information in birth and other registers containing personal data that might disclose the fact of birth out of wedlock should be available only to persons or authorities having a legitimate interest with respect to filiation.

Short birth registration cards instead of birth certificates should generally be used for all children and should be an acceptable document for all purposes that need verification of date and place of birth (such as school registration, employment, voter registration, driver's license). The use of such cards will serve to prevent unwarranted disclosure of potentially embarrassing information about the individual.

The birth registration card should provide the name of the child, the date and place of birth, the sex of the child, the serial number of the record on file, and the date that the original record was filed.

The inclusion of the legitimacy item in a privileged detachable medical health section of the birth certificate and the reporting of this information to the National Center for Health Statistics are considered essential for the protection of the out-of-wedlock child and mother, and for the assessment of incidence and trends of out-of-wedlock births.

8.12 Provision for legitimation

There should be legislative provision to establish the paternity of a child born out of wedlock by reasonable standards of proof in an uncomplicated process that safeguards the privacy of all parties involved, establishes the rights and responsibilities of the unmarried parents, and establishes the legal relationship of the child with the father.

It should be possible to establish the status of a child born out of wedlock as a legitimate child
- through the later marriage of the parents
- by court action
- by acknowledgment of the father in a written statement or public acknowledgment of the child to the community.

8.13 Paternity law

Legislation should provide for action to establish paternity as a civil rather than a criminal procedure, and should permit a father to appear before a court without trial to acknowledge paternity and to agree to provide for the support of his child.

Paternity proceedings should not be mandatory.

The right of the child to know who both the parents are and to have their interest should be the basis for paternity proceedings.

It is desirable for jurisdiction over filiation proceedings to be vested in the juvenile or family court.

There should be provision for a social investigation before a hearing, use of summons, and informal and private hearings.

Effective procedures for collection of support payments should be contained in the paternity law.

8.14 Deprivation of parental rights

There should be legal provision for termination of parental rights in the interest of the child, through proper judicial process, where it has been determined that, even with help of community agencies, the parents in all probability will not be able to perform their parental duties and are either unable or unwilling to relinquish the child.

> Situations in which it should be possible to request termination include those cases of abandonment, neglect, and mental illness in which parents have clearly shown no interest, desire or capacity for giving the child the love, care and protection he needs, and in all probability will not be able to do so; and cases in which they are unable or unwilling to utilize help of community resources in order to do so.

> These instances also include children who have been left in the care of others (including foster care agencies) beyond a stated period of time, and whose parents show either a lack of continuing interest or lack of ability to give proper parental care, protection, and the security of a permanent home.

> In such cases, the rights of the child should take precedence over both the rights and wishes of the parents.

8.15 Legal custody and right to consent to adoption

Concurrent with either relinquishment or termination of parental rights, there should be legally binding action to transfer responsibility for the child to an agency authorized by law to assume both the power and duties of legal custody, and the right to consent to an adoption. (3.20)

> The further consent of the unmarried mother to an adoption should not be required when parental rights have been terminated.

8.16 Compulsory reporting to state welfare department

Statutes providing for compulsory reporting of illegitimate births or pregnancies to the state department of welfare should be enacted only if they can serve to protect the child, to reduce unprotected adoptive placements, and to inform the unmarried mothers about available services. (2.4, 4.15)

> In general, it is undesirable to set up rules for one group that are not equally applicable to others.

> Where such a law is in effect, it is important to interpret it carefully and to have adequate community resources to which referrals can be made.

Responsibility of State Department Administering Social Services

It is the responsibility of a state department administering social services to give leadership in promoting the establishment of and maintenance of adequate services for unmarried parents throughout the state, under both public and voluntary auspices.

8.17 Direct services

The state department responsible for social services should see that all children born out of wedlock and their parents who need direct services are able to receive them, by stimulating and collaborating in

- coordination and full use of existing services
- development of voluntary services
- provision in all geographic areas of public services for those who need them
- enlistment of participation of citizens and representatives of other agencies and organizations in planning and developing of adequate services
- community planning and organization by existing state and local planning bodies, or establishment of such bodies.

8.18 Purchase of care

The state department responsible for social services should be authorized to pay on a per capita basis for needed services or facilities, whether operated under public or voluntary auspices, for children and unwed mothers for whom it has been given responsibility or is otherwise providing services.

When the public agency purchases care, the per capita cost should reflect the actual cost of providing adequate services.

8.19 Information, reporting and statistics

The state department that administers social services should bring together and coordinate all sources of information regarding services available for unmarried parents, data about the extent of the problem and the need for and availability of services throughout the state, and should disseminate such information to all communities. (8.4, 2.5-2.6)

8.20 Research

Research should be carried out to document the extent and demographic characteristics of out-of-wedlock pregnancy and birth for appropriate community plan-

ning to reach and provide services necessary for the parents and children who need them.

8.21 Standard-setting, licensing and consultation

The state department should be required by law to set standards for agencies that care for unmarried parents and their children or provide services to them, and for licensing, inspecting and giving consultative services to agencies, group care facilities and foster family homes for mothers bearing children out of wedlock. (7.2)

8.22 Incorporation of facilities

The state department should give consultation and make recommendations concerning incorporation of child placing and child caring agencies and of group care facilities for mothers bearing children out of wedlock.

SELECTED REFERENCES

Section 0

0.1   *Crisis in Child Mental Health: Challenge of the 70's.* Report of the Joint Commission on the Mental Health of Children. New York, Evanston and London: Harper and Row, 1969.

Cutright, Phillips. Illegitimacy: Myths, Causes and Cures. *Family Planning Perspectives,* January 1971.

Goode, William J. A Policy Paper for Illegitimacy. In *Organizing for Community Welfare,* edited by Mayer N. Zald. Chicago: Quadrangle Books, 1967.

Krause, Harry D. The Non-Marital Child — New Conceptions for the Law of Unlawfulness. *Family Law Quarterly,* June 1967.

Vincent, Clark. *Unmarried Mothers.* Chapter 1. New York: Free Press of Glencoe, 1961.

0.2   Garland, Patricia. Illegitimacy — A Special Minority Group Problem in Urban Areas: New Social Welfare Perspectives. *Child Welfare,* February 1966.

Herzog, Elizabeth. "Unmarried Mothers: Some questions to be answered and some answers to be questioned." In *About the Poor — Some Facts and Some Fictions.* U.S. Department of Health, Education and Welfare, Social and Rehabilitation Service, Children's Bureau, 1967.

Shlakman, Vera. Unmarried Parenthood: An Approach to Social Policy. *Social Casework,* October 1966.

0.3   Herzog. *Op. cit.*

0.5   Campbell, Arthur A. The Role of Family Planning in the Reduction of Poverty. Journal of Marriage and the Family, May 1968.

Cutright. *Op. cit.*

Herzog. *Op. cit.*

Kronick, Jane Collier. An Assessment of Research Knowledge Concerning the Unmarried Mother. In *The Unwed Mother,* edited by Robert W. Roberts. New York and London: Harper and Row, 1966.

0.6   Chaskel, Ruth. Illegitimacy — The Dimensions of Prevention. *Social Casework,* February 1969.

Cutright. *Op. cit.*

Pope, Hallowell. Unwed Mothers and Their Sex Partners. *Journal of Marriage and Family,* August 1967.

Section 1

1.3   Gallagher, Ursula. *Comprehensive Services for the Unmarried Parent.* Washington, D.C.: Office of Child Development, U.S. Department of Health, Education and Welfare, 1969.

Section 2

2.1   Garrell, Dale C. A Hotline Telephone Service for Young People in Crisis. *Children,* November-December 1969.

2.2   McMurray, Georgia L. Community Action on Behalf of Pregnant School-Age Girls: Educational Policies and Beyond. *Child Welfare,* June 1970.

Pannor, Reuben; Massarik, Fred; Evans, Byron, *The Unmarried Father.* Chapter IV. New York: Springer, 1971.

2.3   Olander, Jeanne. The Single Parent and Her Baby — Implications for Community Action. San Francisco: Report of the Single Parent Project, financed by a grant of the San Francisco Foundation, administered by the Board of Directors of the Florence Crittenton Home.

2.4   Herzog, Elizabeth, "Unmarried Mothers: The Service Gap Revisited." *Children,* May-June 1968.

Lewis, Richard L., Jr. The Unmarried Parent and Community Resources. *Child Welfare,* December 1968.

Section 3

3.3   Roulet, Norman. Group Psychotherapy With Unmarried Mothers. In *The Double Jeopardy, The Triple Crisis: Illegitimacy Today.* New York: National Council on Illegitimacy, 1969.

Dawdy, Arletta. Group Services for Teenage Mothers. *Ibid.*

3.4   Bernstein, Rose. *Helping Unmarried Mothers.* New York: Association Press, 1971.

3.7   Friedman, Helen L. The Mother-Daughter Relationship: Its Potential in Treatment of Young Unwed Mothers. *Social Case-work,* October 1966.

3.8   Dame, Nenabelle G.; Finck, George H.; Mayos, Ruth G.; Reiner, Beatrice Simcox; Smith, Brady O. Conflict in Marriage Following Premarital Pregnancy. *American Journal of Orthopsychiatry,* March 1966.

3.9   *Family Planning Evaluation, Abortion Surveillance Report – Legal Abortions, United States Annual Summary, 1970.* Atlanta: Epidemiology Program, Family Planning Evaluation Activity, Center for Disease Control, Public Health Service, Health Services and Mental Health Administration, U.S. Department of Health, Education and Welfare, 1971.

Potts, Leah. Counseling Women With Unwanted Pregnancies. In *Family Planning – A Source Book and Case Material for Social Work Education,* edited by Florence Haselkorn in consultation with Katherine Oettinger. New York: Council on Social Work Education, 1971.

3.10   A Guide for Collaboration of Physician, Social Worker and Lawyer in Helping the Unmarried Mother. *Child Welfare,* April 1967.

3.11   Bernstein. *Op. cit.*

Festinger, Trudy Bradley. Unwed Mothers and Their Decisions to Keep or Surrender Children. *Child Welfare,* April 1971.

3.13   Olander, Jeanne. The Single Parent and Her Baby: Implications for Community Action. San Francisco: A report of the Single Parent Project, 1967.

Sauber, Mignon, and Corrigan, Eileen M. *The Six-Year Experience of Unwed Mothers as Parents: A Continuing Study of These Mothers and Their Children.* New York: Research Department, Community Council of Greater New York, 1970.

Reed, Ellery F. Unmarried Mothers Who Kept Their Babies. *Children,* May-June, 1965.

3.18   *Legislative guides for the termination of parental rights and responsibilities and the adoption of children.* Washington, D.C.: Children's Bureau, Social Security Administration, 19▢1.

3.21   Bernstein, *Op. cit.*

3.24   Burgess, Linda C. The Unmarried Father in Adoption Planning. *Children,* March-April, 1968.

LaBarre, Maurine, and LaBarre, Weston. "The Triple Crisis: Adolescence, Early Mar-riage, and Parenthood." In *The Double Jeopardy, The Triple Crisis: Illegitimacy Today.* New York: National Council on Illegitimacy, 1969.

3.23   Bernstein. *Op. cit.*

LaBarre. *Op. cit.*

Pannor, Reuben; Massarik, Fred; Evans, Byron. *The Unmarried Father: New Approaches for Helping Unmarried Young Parents.* Chapter IV. New York: Springer, 1971.

3.27   Bernstein. *Op. cit.*

Khlentzos, Michael T., and Pagliaro, Mary A. Observations From Psychotherapy With Unwed Mothers. *American Journal of Orthopsychiatry,* July 1965.

Section 4

4.8   Lin-fu, Jane S. *Neonatal Narcotic Addiction.* Washington, D.C.: Division of Health Services, Children's Bureau, Welfare Administration, U. S. Department of Health, Education and Welfare, 1967.

4.9   Family Planning: The Role of Social Work, edited by Florence Haselkorn. In *Perspectives in Social Work, Vol. 2, No. 1.* Garden City, N.Y.: Adelphi University School of Social Work, 1968.

Gray, Naomi Thomas. Family Planning and Social Welfare's Responsibility. *Social Case-work,* October 1966.

Meier, Gitta. Implementing the Objectives of Family Planning Programs. In *Family Planning: A Source Book and Case Material for Social Work Education,* edited by Florence Haselkorn in consultation with Katherine Oettinger. New York: Council on Social Work Education, 1971.

4.22   Infant Mortality Rates by Legitimacy Status – U.S. 1964-66. In *Monthly Vital Statistics Report,* Vol. 20, 5th supplement. National Natality and Infant Mortality Surveys, 1964-66. U.S. Department of Health, Education and Welfare, Public Health Services.

Section 5

5.7   A Guide for Collaboration of Physician, Social Worker and Lawyer in Helping the Unmarried Mother and Her Child. *Child Welfare,* April 1967.

Bernstein, Bernice L. Law as an Instrument of Justice for Unwed Parents. In *Unmarried Parenthood – Clues to Agency and Community Action.* New York: National Council on Illegitimacy, 1967.

5.9   Terkelson, Helen E. *Counseling the Unwed Mother.* Englewood Cliffs, N.J.: Prentice-Hall, 1964.

5.19   McDowell, John. The Clergy's Role in Social Action. In *The Double Jeopardy, the Triple Crisis – Illegitimacy Today.* New York: National Council on Illegitimacy, 1969.

Section 6

6.13   *Unwed Mothers: Report on Services, Financial and Client Data for 1969.* Prepared by Jean Bedger. Florence Crittenton Association of America, 1970.

6.14   The Changing Role of Maternity Homes. NCI Newsletter, Fall 1968.

6.15   Conner, Leora L. An Extended Service – A Half-way House for Unwed Mothers. *Child Welfare,* April 1966.

Henry, Sue. Mutual Care Home. *The Junior League,* July-August 1970.

Section 7

7.3   Verner, Major Mary E. Administrative Concepts in Comprehensive Services for Unmarried Parents. In *Unmarried Parenthood – Clues to Agency and Community Action.* New York: National Council on Illegitimacy, 1967.

7.5   Lewis, Richard L., Jr. The Unmarried Parent and Community Resources, *Child Welfare,* December 1968.

7.6   Insley, Virginia. Some Recent Legislation for Social Work. In *Mothers at Risk: The Role of Social Work in Prevention of Morbidity in Infants of Socially Disadvantaged Mothers,* edited by Florence Haselkorn. Garden City, N.Y.: Adelphi University School of Social Work, 1966.

7.7   *Beginning Community-wide Services on a Non-Residential Basis for Pregnant*

School-Age Girls. Chicago: Florence Crittenton Association. Prepared by Mary Watson Palmer.

7.13   *An Accounting Manual for Voluntary Social Welfare Organizations.* New York: Child Welfare League of America, Family Service Association of America, Travelers Aid Association of America, 1971.

7.23   Schlosser, Donald H. How Volunteers Can Strengthen Child Welfare Services. *Child Welfare,* October 1969.

7.39   Klerman, Lorraine V. The Potential Contribution of Research Projects to Comprehensive Programs for Pregnant Adolescents. In *Illegitimacy: Changing Services for Changing Times.* New York: National Council on Illegitimacy, 1970.

Section 8

8.1   *Beginning Community-wide Services on a Non-Residential Basis* for Pregnant School-Age Girls. Florence Crittenton Association of America.

8.6   Howard, Marion. Comprehensive Service Programs for School-Age Pregnant Girls. *Children,* September-October 1968.

8.8   Filas, Francis L., S.J. Sex Education and the Prevention of Illegitimacy. In *Unmarried Parenthood: Clues to Agency and Community Action.* New York: National Council on Illegitimacy, 1967.

McMurray, Georgia L. Community Action on Behalf of Pregnant School-Age Girls: Educational Policies and Beyond. *Child Welfare,* June 1970.

Reynolds, Harriet Blackburn. Educational Services for Unmarried Mothers – A Program Model. In *Effective Services for Unmarried Parents and Their Children: Innovative Community Approaches.* New York: National Council on Illegitimacy, 1968.

8.12   Krause, Harry D. *Illegitimacy: Law and Social Policy.* Indianapolis, Kansas City, New York: Bobbs-Merrill, 1971.

INDEX

A

Abortion, counseling about, 3.9; differential use of, 0.5; medical discussion of, 3.9

Acknowledgment of paternity, 8.8, 8.9

Activities, educational, 6.21

Administration, and organization of services, 7.1-7.42; responsibility of hospital, 4.14

Admission policy in group living facility, 6.23

Adolescent, dating patterns, 0.5; social work with, 3.21

Adoptions, early relinquishment for, 3.15; independent, in hospitals, 4.19; right to consent to, 8.15

Age, distribution by, 0.4

Agency, financial resources, 7.12-7.16; manual, 7.18; organization and administration, 7.1-7.42; planning and coordination, 7.7; purposes and objectives of, 7.3; relation to the community, 7.5; responsibility for interpretation, 7.41-7.42; responsibility for promotion of legislation, 7.8; responsibility for social action, 7.6; standards of service, 7.4

Assistance, financial, 5.13; in living arrangements, 6.4

Assumptions underlying practice, 0.7

Attorney, role of, 5.7

Auspices, of agency services, 7.1; of group living facility, 6.13

Authorization of agency service, 7.2

B

Baby, in hospital, care of, 4.11; pediatric care of, 4.8; relinquishment of, 3.15-3.18

Birth records, 8.11

Births, number and rate of out-of-wedlock, 0.3

Board of directors, composition of, 7.10; qualifications of, 7.11; responsibilities of, 7.9

Brochures, interpretation through, 2.6

Buildings and grounds, of group living facility, 6.28-6.29

C

Care, day, 5.16, 6.17; medical, 4.1-4.22; of baby in hospital, 4.11; of the child, 1.3; payment for hospital, 4.13; pediatric, 4.8; postpartum, 4.7; prenatal, 4.5; purchase of, 8.18; source of medical, 4.3; standards for medical, 4.4

Case records, compilation of, 7.34; confidentiality of, 7.36; preservation of, 7.35

Casework, use of, 3.3

Characteristics of group residence care, 6.12

Child, care of, 1.3; decision to keep, 3.12; foster family care of, 3.14; help in planning for, 3.11; keeping, 3.13; legal custody of, 8.15; payment for, 7.15; protection of, 3.10; relinquishing, 3.15-3.20; rights of, 8.9; separation from, 3.17; social work responsibility in planning for, 3.10-3.20; support of, 3.10, 3.26, 6.24, 7.15, 8.13

Clergyman, interpretation to, 2.6; role of, 5.9

Collection of support payments, 8.13

Community, agency relation to, 7.5; coordination with other services, 5.12; health agencies in, 4.22; interpretation, 7.41-7.42; planning and coordination, 8.1; responsibility for interpretation of services, 8.3; responsibility for legislation, 8.9-8.16

Community organization, use of, 3.3

Companion homes, 6.9

Composition of the board, 7.10

Compulsory reporting, reaching mother through, 2.4; to state welfare department, 8.16

Confidentiality, 2.3, 7.36; in hospital, 4.18; in research, 7.39

Group homes, 6.15

Group living facility, 6.11-6.29; admission to, 6.23; auspices of, 6.13; buildings and grounds of, 6.28, 6.29; characteristics of, 6.12; cooperative living arrangements of, 6.16; day care in, 6.17; education in, 6.21; group homes as, 6.15; licensing of, 6.18; maternity homes as, 6.14; medical and hospital care in, 6.22; payments for, 6.24; social work in, 6.20; staff of, 6.27; use of, 6.11, 6.19

Group work, use of, 3.3

H

Health, agencies, 4.22; requirements for, in group living facility, 6.18; responsibility for meeting needs of, 4.1

Help in planning for the child, 3.11

Homemaker services, 5.18

Hospital, and adoptions, 4.19; education of staff in, 4.16; in group living facility, 6.22; medical report from, 4.22; nursery care of babies in, 4.11; payment for, 4.13; referrals to agency, 4.15; responsibility of, 4.14-4.21; services, 4.5, 4.13-4.21; social worker in, 4.12, 4.21

Hospitalization at time of delivery, 4.6

House rules, in group living facility, 6.25

I

Incorporation of facilities by state department, 8.22

Independent adoptions and hospital, 4.19

Independent mother, special needs of, 3.22

Individuals for whom services are appropriate, 1.2

Infants, day care of, 6.17; in group living facilities, 6.18; leaving hospital, 4.11; residential group care of, 3.14

Information, and referral services, 8.4; from state department, 8.19; to public through the use of mass media, 2.5

Initial contact for service, 3.4; by the agency, 2.4; with family, 3.7

Initial participation of family members, 3.7

Integration of social work and medical services, 4.2

Interpretation of services, agency responsibility for, 7.41-7.42; community responsibility for, 8.3; purpose of, 7.3; to key groups, 2.6; use of mass media in, 2.5

Involving the father, 1.2, 3.24; purpose of, 2.2

J

Job definitions, 7.19

Jurisdiction, in licensing, 6.18; over paternity proceedings, 8.13

K

Keeping the child, 3.12-3.14; in own home, 3.13

Key groups, interpretation to, 2.6

L

Leaflets, use of, 2.6

Legal, custody of child, 8.15; proceedings against father, 3.25; rights of parents, 3.10; services, 3.13, 1.3; status of minors, 8.10

Legal status of minor unmarried parent, 8.10

Legislation, agency promotion of, 7.8; community responsibility for, 8.9-8.16

Legitimation, provision for, 8.12

Licensing, of group living facilities, 6.18; state department responsibility for, 8.21

Living arrangements, in companion and wage homes, 6.9; in cooperative arrangement, 6.16; in foster families, 6.5; in group homes, 6.15; in group living facility, 6.11; in maternity home, 6.14; in own apartment, 6.3; in own family, 6.2; selection of, 6.1; use of, 6.11, 6.19
Location of group living facility, 6.29

M

Maintaining own apartment, 6.3
Manual, agency, 7.18
Mass media, use of, 2.5
Maternity homes, 6.14
Medical and hospital care, 4.1-4.21; and social work, 4.10-4.13; basic requirements for, 4.4; in group living facility, 6.22; integration with social work services, 4.2
Medical profession, interpretation to, 2.6; responsibility for meeting health needs, 4.1
Medical report from hospital, 4.20
Medical services, 4.1-4.21; and social work, 4.10-4.13; in group living facility, 6.22; integration with social work, 4.2
Mentally deficient unmarried mother, protection for child of, 3.11
Methods, social work, 3.3
Minors, legal status of, 8.10; medical consent from parents of, 3.8, 4.5; services to, 2.3
Multiple service organizations, 8.6

N

Nature of problem, 0.1
Need for, special measures for reaching out to unmarried parent, 2.1; specialized services, 0.1, 0.2
Needs, individual, of the unmarried father, 3.23; of the independent mother, 3.22
Number of out-of-wedlock births, 0.3
Nurse, role of, 5.5
Nutritionist, role of, 5.11

O

Office staff, 7.30
Older unmarried mother, 3.12, 3.13
Organization and administration of services, 7.1-7.42
Other community services, 5.12-5.19
Other services and resources, use of, 5.1-5.19
Own family, living with, 6.2
Own home, keeping child in, 3.13

P

Parent-child homes, 6.10
Parental rights and responsibilities, 3.10
Participation, of agency in community planning, 8.1, 7.7; of staff in policy and procedures, 7.17
Participation in social planning, 7.6-7.8
Participation of family members, initial, 3.7
Paternity, law, 8.13; proceedings to establish, 3.25, 8.12
Patterns and solutions to problems accompanying pregnancy out of wedlock, 0.5
Payments, basis and size of, 7.16; for boarding care of child, 7.15; for child, 3.10, 3.26, 7.15, 8.13; for foster family care, 6.8; for hospital care, 4.13; for residential care, 6.24; for services, 7.15; in group living, 6.24
Pediatric care of the baby, 4.8
Personal qualifications of foster parents, 6.7

Personality, understanding of adolescent, 3.21
Personnel, differential use of, 7.22
Personnel policies, 7.31
Physical plan of group living facility, 6.28
Physicians, and independent adoptions, 4.19; interpretation to, 2.6; qualifications of, 7.32; role of, 4.2-4.9, 5.4
Planning, and coordination of agency service, 7.7; and coordination of community services, 8.1; for the child, social work assistance in, 3.10-3.20; for the child in the hospital, 4.11; for termination of service, 3.6; in community, 7.5; social, participation in, 7.6-7.8; with hospital, 4.12; with other community services, 5.12; with specialist, 5.2
Policies, 6.23-6.26; and procedures of group living facility, 6.23-6.26; and procedures of social agency, 7.17-7.18; for use of specialists, 7.33
Postpartum care of the mother, 4.7
Practices, assumptions underlying, 0.7
Pregnancy out of wedlock, patterns and solutions of, 0.5
Premarital counseling, 3.8
Prenatal care, 4.5
Preservation of records, 7.35
Prevention of out-of-wedlock births, 0.6
Problem, extent of, 0.2; nature of, 0.1
Protection, of finality of relinquishment, 3.19; of rights of child, 8.9, 3.10
Provision, for legitimation, 8.12; of funds for services, 8.7
Psychiatrist, role of, 5.6
Psychologist, role of, 5.8
Public and voluntary cooperation, 8.2
Public health agencies, services of, 4.2, 4.6-4.9, 4.22
Public relations program, 2.5, 2.6, 7.41, 7.42
Purchase, of care, 8.18; of service, 7.14
Purposes, and objectives of agency, 7.3; of interpretation, 7.41; of reaching out, 2.2; of services, 1.1

Q

Qualifications, of board membership, 7.11; of executive director, 7.27; of foster family, 6.7; of social work staff, 7.21; of specialists, 7.32; of staff in group living facility, 6.25; of supervisory staff, 7.28

R

Rate of out-of-wedlock births, 0.3
Reaching the unmarried parents, conditions for, 2.3; need for special measures for, 2.1; purpose of, 2.2
Records, birth, 8.11; case, 7.34; preservation of, 7.35
Referral, between social agency and hospital, 4.3, 4.10, 4.11, 4.15; information service and, 8.4; to other agency or resource, 2.3, 5.12-5.19
Reformatory, use of for unmarried mothers, 2.3
Related resources, use of, 1.3, 5.12-5.19
Relationship, of child with father, 8.12; continuity of, 1.4
Religious, convictions about abortion, 3.9; counselor, role of, 5.9
Relinquishing the child, 3.15-3.20; early, 3.15; emotional readiness for, 3.16
Remaining with own family, 6.2
Reporting, and statistics, 7.37, 7.38; information and statistics, 8.19
Requirements, for health and safety of group facility, 6.18; for medical care, 4.4-4.9
Research, agency responsibility for, 7.39; confidentiality in, 7.39; funds for, 7.40; state department role in, 8.20
Residential group care, characteristics of, 6.12
Resources, financial, 7.12-7.16; use of related, 1.3, 5.12-5.19

Respect for the mother's wishes, 4.17

Responsibility, duration of parental, 3.20; during prenatal period, 4.10; for agency policy, 7.17; for meeting health needs, 4.1; for research, 7.39; for social action, 7.6; for support by father, 3.26, 8.13; for support by mother, 3.10, 6.22; in planning for the child, 3.11-3.20; of board, 7.9; of community health agencies, 4.22; of group living facility, 6.19-6.20; of hospital, 4.14-4.21; of hospital administration, 4.14; of social agency, 1.4; of social worker in hospital, 4.21; of state department, 8.17-8.22; of state board of education, 8.8

Rights, deprivation of parental, 8.14; of child and parent, 8.9, 0.1, 3.10; of minors, 8.10; to consent to adoption, 8.15

S

Safety requirements in group facility, 6.18

Schools, cooperation with, 5.14; coordination with, 2.4; interpretation to, 2.6

Selection, of hospital, 4.6; of living arrangements, 6.1

Separation from the child, 3.17

Services, appropriate individuals for, 1.2; basis for, 3.5; community, coordination with, 5.12-5.19; costs of, 7.13; direct, from state department, 8.17; expansion of, 8.5; family planning, 4.9, 5.17; for minors, 8.10; in hospital, 4.5, 4.13-4.21; information and referral, 8.4; informing public about, 2.5, 2.6; initial contact for, 3.4; integration of medical and social work, 4.2; purchase of, 7.14; purpose of, 1.1

Size, of staff, 7.20; of workload, 7.24

Social action, responsibility for, 7.6

Social agency, auspices of, 7.1; authorization of, 7.2; board of, 7.9-7.11; community interpretation by, 7.41, 7.42; financial resources of, 7.12-7.16; group facility as, 6.13; organization of, 7.1-7.11; planning and coordination, 7.7; policies and procedures of, 7.17-7.18, 7.33; referral by hospital to, 4.14; responsibility of, 1.4; staffing of, 7.19-7.23

Social work, and medical services, 4.10-4.13; goals, 3.1; in group living facility, 6.20; in planning for child, 3.10-3.20; methods of, 3.3; responsibility to assist unmarried parents, 3.8, 3.9; with adolescent, 3.21; with family, 3.7, 3.27; with independent mother, 3.22; with unmarried father, 3.23-3.26; with unmarried mother and father, 1.3, 3.1-3.7; with unmarried parents, 3.1-3.7

Social worker, in hospital, 4.12, 4.21; qualifications of, 7.29

Socioeconomic group, 0.2, 0.5

Source, of agency funds, 7.12; of medical care, 4.3

Specialists, policies for use of, 7.33; qualifications of, 7.32; use of by parent, 5.2

Specialized services, need for, 0.1, 0.2

Staff, development, 7.25, 7.26; education in hospital, 4.16; in group living facility, 6.27; office, 7.30; qualifications for social work, 7.21; size of, 7.20; supervisory, 7.28

Staffing, 7.19-7.24

Standards, of agency services, 7.4; of medical care, 4.4; setting by state department, 8.21

State department responsibility, for direct services, 8.17; for incorporation of facilities, 8.22; for information, reporting and statistics, 8.19; for licensing, consultation and standards, 6.18, 8.21; for purchase of care, 8.18; for research, 8.20

Statistics, and reporting by agency, 7.37-7.38; information and reporting of by state department, 8.19

Study of foster family homes, 6.6

Supervision, of foster family homes, 6.6; of staff, 7.26

Supervisory staff, 7.28

Support of child, by father, 3.26, 8.13; by mother, 3.10, 6.22

Surrender of child, 3.15-3.20

T

Termination, of parental rights, 3.18; of pregnancy, 3.9; of service, 3.6

Total service, 1.3

Training schools, use of, 2.3

U

Unmarried fathers, acknowledgment of child by, 8.12, 8.13; decision to involve, 3.24; individual needs and problems of, 3.23; legal proceedings against, 3.25; responsibility of, for support by, 3.26, 8.13

Unmarried mothers, distribution by age, 0.4; minor, 8.10; respect for wishes of, 4.17; responsibility for support, 3.10, 6.22; rights of, 3.10; special needs of independent, 3.22

Unmarried parent, adolescent, 3.21; definition of, 1.2; reaching, 2.1-2.6; rights and responsibilities of, 3.10; services for, 1.3; social work with, 3.1-3.7, 1.3

V

Vocational counseling, 5.15
Volunteers, use of, 7.23

W

Wage homes, 6.9
Work, assignments in group living facility, 6.26
Workloads, 7.24